Emotional Lite

One of the five books in the *Me* … teachers and other professionals working with chil… on the topic of 'Emotional Literacy' and how to support children and young people … of self-discovery where they learn to recognise, understand, share and manage a range of emotions. Promoting a proactive rather than a reactive approach to dealing with the social and emotional aspects of learning and managing the world of today, *Emotional Literacy* addresses the increasing number of mental health issues arising among young people.

Chapters span key topics including Recognising Emotions, Understanding Emotions, Self-Regulation and Empathy. This book offers:

- Easy to follow and flexible lesson plans that can be adapted and personalised for use in lessons, smaller groups or 1:1 work.
- Resources that are linked to the PSHE and Wellbeing curriculum for KS1, KS2 and KS3.
- New research, 'Circles for Learning', where the introduction of baby observation into the classroom by a teacher is used to understand and develop self-awareness, skills for learning, relationships, neuroscience and awareness of others.
- Sections on the development of key skills in communication, skills for learning, collaboration, empathy and self-confidence.
- Learning links, learning objectives and reflection questions.

Offering research-driven, practical strategies and lesson plans, *Emotional Literacy* is an essential resource book for educators and health professionals looking to have a positive impact on the mental health and wellbeing of the children in their care; both now and in the future.

Alison Waterhouse has worked in mainstream, special education and the independent sector for the past 30 years, specialising in working with children with AEN including Mental Health and Wellbeing. She has set up and developed an Independent Therapeutic Special School and developed a role as Teacher in Charge of the Social and Emotional Wellbeing of the Whole School Community, has been an Inclusion Manager and Deputy Head in mainstream schools. She now works as an Independent Educational Consultant for SEN and Wellbeing, is involved in staff training and has her own Educational Psychotherapy practice. Alison works with children who are referred due to difficulties with self-esteem, anger, anxiety, depression and other Mental Health needs as well as children with other learning differences. Alison is developing the Circles for Learning Project in schools, has already undertaken a Primary Research Project and is now working on a Secondary Research Project. The resources were put together to support staff with these projects.

Emotional literacy
Self-discovery
Skills for effective learning in school
Positive relationships in school
The brain and learning
The invisible roots of learning

Emotional Literacy

Supporting Emotional Health and Wellbeing in School

Alison Waterhouse

LONDON AND NEW YORK

First published 2019
by Routledge
2 Park Square, Milton Park, Abingdon, Oxon OX14 4RN

and by Routledge
52 Vanderbilt Avenue, New York, NY 10017

Routledge is an imprint of the Taylor & Francis Group, an informa business

British Library Cataloguing-in-Publication Data
A catalogue record for this book is available from the British Library

Library of Congress Cataloging-in-Publication Data
A catalog record for this book has been requested

ISBN: 978-1-138-37027-2 (pbk)
ISBN: 978-0-429-42809-8 (ebk)

Typeset in Avant Garde
by Apex CoVantage, LLC

From Mummy Bean to Baby Bean,

I love you to the Moon and back.

Contents

Introduction

EMOTIONAL COMPETENCIES

Developing emotional literacy is now seen as being increasingly important to the development of children and young people. In schools, the term 'emotional literacy' is widely used and is underpinned by a range of traditional views on intelligence. These traditional views suggested that intelligence was something that you were born with and therefore unchangeable but that it could be measured by various IQ tests. In the 1980s, Howard Gardner proposed that intelligence should have a much broader definition (Gardner and Hatch 1989). From this emerged the theory that people must be 'emotionally intelligent'. This term has continued to be defined by academics.

Some people believe that emotional intelligence involves perception, integration, understanding and management of emotion (Mayer Cobb 2000) and that it is an ability. Goleman defined emotional intelligence as self-awareness, self-regulation, motivation, empathy and social skills (Goleman 2004). This continued the debate as to whether it is a skill or an ability. For educators, the term 'emotional literacy' may have come to be used because 'emotional intelligence' had been seen as unchangeable. Weare (2004) uses the term 'emotional competencies', which include the ability to understand, express and manage our own emotions and respond to the emotions of others.

Research clearly shows that teaching emotional competencies within schools has a wide range of educational and social benefits including greater educational and work success, improved behaviour, increased inclusion, improved learning, greater social cohesion, increased social capital and improvements in mental health. Schools are not just dispensers of knowledge but are in essence a social place of learning and so the organisation is a natural environment for academic learning, social learning and emotional learning.

Learning is so interwoven with emotions and the ability to work with others that learning and social and emotional competencies cannot be separated from the academic learning task. Learning involves neurological processes, social interaction and the ability to manage emotions. These three strands run throughout all that we learn, and have to be managed by the learner. At times our emotional responses to learning, or the learning interaction, can overwhelm our cognitive processes and thus prevent effective learning.

To be an effective learner, a wealth of emotions has to be managed and regulated. Children enter the learning environment with an array of different experiences and beliefs created from their interaction with the world and the people they have met within it. These experiences have already influenced them, and have had an effect on their learning. Have they learnt that it is safe to be curious and ask questions? Is learning a pleasurable thing or is this an area that is fraught with danger? Have they been encouraged to find out about the world in which they live or have they been shut down? Is making a mistake a step to succeeding or is it something that is punished and frowned upon? Is it safe to take risks? Has their experience been of an adult there to support them or of trying to manage on their own? Is it safe to ask for help or is it something that they have learnt will get them shouted at or ignored? These are just some of the many emotions that children have to regulate and manage. If the emotions are overwhelming then they will create barriers to learning. Emotions often operate the on–off switch for learning and so, by teaching children and young people about emotions and ways of managing them, they are more able to manage the learning task.

Research has demonstrated that young people show enhanced social and emotional learning skills and attitudes and positive social behaviour following interventions that support emotional competencies, as well as fewer conduct problems and lower levels of emotional distress. Good emotional competencies are associated with greater wellbeing and better school performance. If children and young people are not able to manage emotions then a variety of difficulties can emerge.

The resources and lesson ideas found in this book all come from Alison Waterhouse's own work as a Head of a Therapeutic school, SENCo and Educational Psychotherapist or from colleagues who have undertaken the Circles for Learning Project with their own classes. They are inspired by a range of approaches including Psychodynamic, Solution Focused, Cognitive Behaviour Therapy and Learning to Learn. All are focused on developing children and young people's understanding of self. This includes how their sense of self has developed, why they think as they do and, most importantly, how to create the energy and skills to change or grow – thus giving children and young people a sense of efficacy.

The resources are laid out in such a way that they are a guide book full of ideas and places to visit and explore, and not a scheme of work to be religiously followed. All class teachers have a wealth of knowledge and understanding about children and young people and it is important both to recognise and to use these skills and expertise. Because of their knowledge and understanding of the children and young people they work with, they are best placed to know and understand which areas their children need to explore and develop, discuss and question.

This is a resource book for practitioners who wish to share in a rich and exciting journey with children and young people in their care. The resources are written for professionals working with children and young people as a way of developing strong foundations for Mental Health and Wellbeing. This includes teachers, ELSAs, TAs, learning mentors, school counsellors and therapists. The lessons can be used to support the Circles for Learning Project or as a standalone resource supporting the positive development of Mental Health and Wellbeing. When the text uses the term 'class baby', this is referring to the baby (and parent) visiting a classroom as part of the Circles for Learning Project. For classes and schools not able to use this project, photos or videos could be used to help the children think about the opening questions or, alternatively, this part can be omitted, and the task can become the starting point for the lesson.

THE CIRCLES FOR LEARNING PROJECT

Circles for Learning is a unique, research-based, whole class or small group project that builds the positive foundations for Mental Health and Wellbeing. It supports and strengthens learning skills alongside the development of social skills, emotional literacy and wellbeing. It facilitates and encourages children to experience how learning happens and explore brain development, relationships and emotions. This includes how other people might feel or experience situations, how to manage emotions, discover our sense of self and understand how our beliefs influence our behaviour.

Circles for Learning has been developed by Alison Waterhouse over the past five years. Alison initiated the Circles for Learning Project in primary schools in East Sussex, where she led and developed this innovative way of working with children. As colleagues became aware of her work, they asked to get involved, so Alison set up the Primary Research Project for five schools in East Sussex where she worked closely with the class teachers to both design and develop the project in their schools. This enabled her to work in both small rural schools and very deprived large urban schools as well as with a variety of teachers. As a result of the interest of professionals in the Secondary field, Alison has just completed a research project with 4 different secondary schools to explore and measure the impact of the work within their environment. This work has been the core of a research MA in Education with the University of York.

The project trains and then supports teachers to bring a parent and baby into the classroom once a month for a year. The children and young people are supported in observing the interactions, learning, relationships and the baby's early developing sense of self. Then, with the support of the teacher, they explore and think about what they have seen and how this may link to their own development, thinking, behaviour and ways of interacting with others.

These observations are the provocation or stimulus to follow-up work led by the teacher exploring one of the Circles for Learning's five areas of work:

1. Emotional competencies: including recognising emotions, managing our own emotions, recognising emotions in others and developing strategies to cope and deal with these emotions.

2. Relationships: including social skills, the learning relationship, social inclusion and empathy.

3. Self-discovery: including self-concept, self-esteem, self-efficacy, self-regulation, self-talk, self-compassion, mindsets and resilience.

4. Skills for effective learning.

5. Neuroscience and learning.

These five key areas form the foundations for Mental Health and Wellbeing. The follow-up work is not a scheme of work to be followed regardless of the needs of the children and young

people but a wide range of activities that the teacher can refer to and use that supports the needs of the group at that time.

The resources within each of the five books in the *Mental Health and Wellbeing Toolkit* can be used as standalone resources to support the five key areas that create the foundations for Mental Health and Wellbeing or as part of the Circles for Learning Project.

TRACKING SHEET

NAME/GROUP:		
DATE:		TERM:
ASSESSMENTS UNDERTAKEN:		OTHER INFORMATION:
Date	Lesson:	Comments
Date	Lesson:	Comments
Date	Lesson:	Comments
Date	Lesson:	Comments
Date	Lesson:	Comments
Date	Lesson:	Comments
Date	Lesson:	Comments
Date	Lesson:	Comments
Date	Lesson:	Comments
Date	Lesson:	Comments

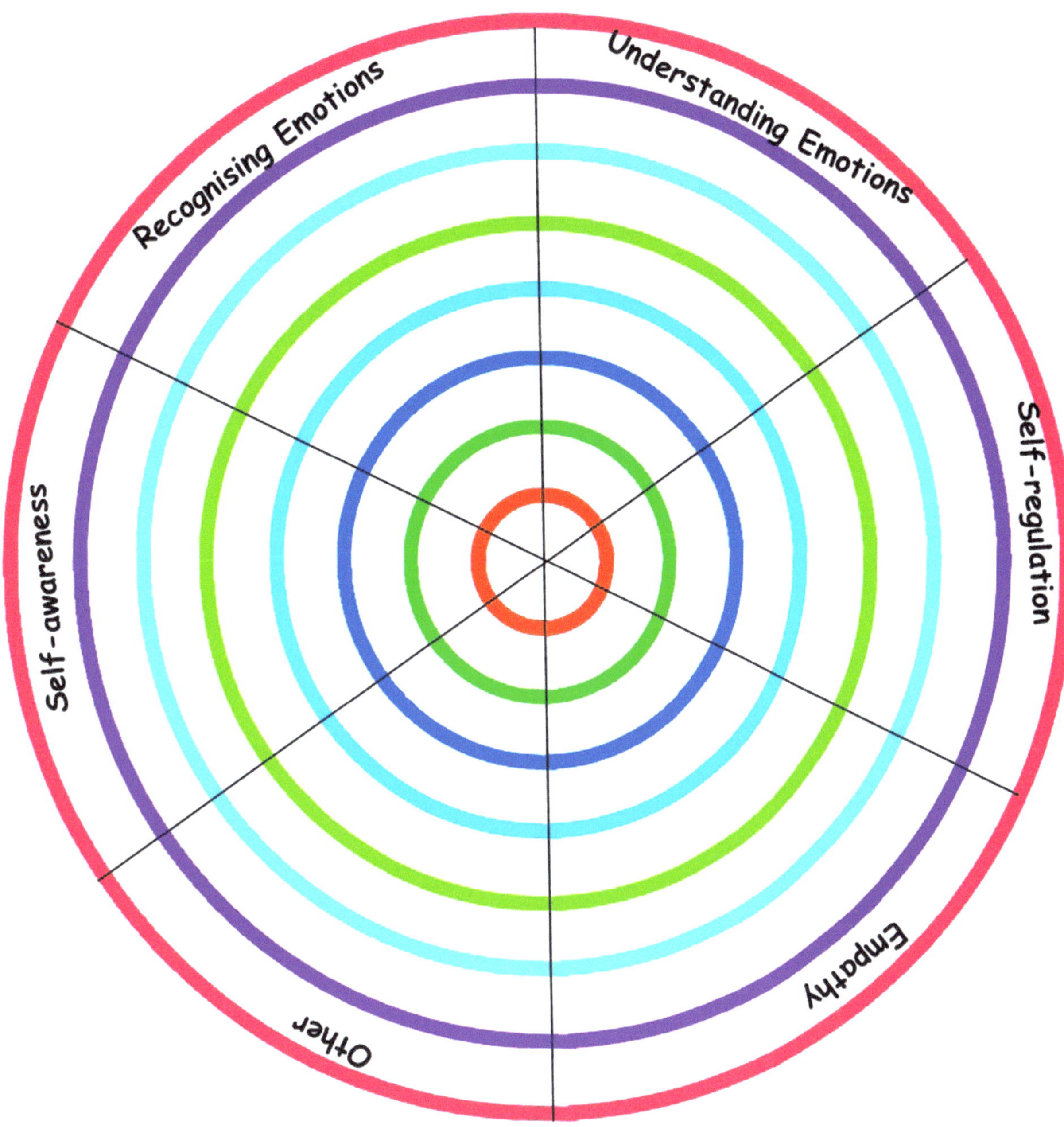

The circular tracking document has been designed to allow practitioners to monitor and track the areas that they have covered with the children. As each lesson is covered they are entered onto the document within the focus section. This enables practitioners to see the particular focus they are taking with their group. For some classes they may present a high need within a particular area or a strength in another area and so this can be shown and monitored. The document also allows for other lessons/activities to be added to the document that may have extended knowledge and understanding in this area from PSHE or Circle Time focus.

The document allows the flexibility to meet the needs of the children as they arise rather than having to follow a pre-set curriculum and in so doing allows practitioners to clearly see the areas of need and what they are doing to meet them.

Chapter 1

Recognising emotions

What is an emotion?

SESSION OBJECTIVES

To identify a range of emotions and describe how they make the body feel.

To be able to describe an event that may have caused an emotion.

SESSION OUTCOMES

- ✓ To be able to identify a range of emotions and describe the features of the person affected by these displays.
- ✓ To be able to describe how an emotion makes their body feel.

LESSON PLAN

- ➢ To support the children and young people in identifying the range of emotions that their class baby exhibited when they visited.
- ➢ To support the children and young people in describing what they observed about parent or baby in relation to their emotions.

For those classrooms not able to undertake the Circles for Learning Project, video clips or photographs can be used to support the discussion around the topic and stimulate thoughts and ideas from the children and young people.

Task

KS1: To play Emotional Charades.
KS2/3: To create a picture depicting an emotion.
KS3: To create a game to teach younger children about emotions.

KS1

1. Share photographs of people showing strong emotions.
2. Ask the children to observe and then describe what they can see – mouth wide and turned up at the edges with teeth showing, crinkled lines around the eyes, eyes sparkling and twinkling.

3. Ask the children what the emotion is.

4. Ask the children to think of a time when they felt this emotion – share stories about the time.

5. Ask them how it made their body feel – list the words under the emotion on the board – tingly, warm, soft, relaxed, light, energised.

6. Divide the children into groups and give them each an emotion: Sad, Angry, Happy, Frightened, Excited, Jealous, Worried.

7. Ask them to:

    - Draw a person feeling this feeling.
    - Write how this feeling makes their bodies feel – one word on a sticky note.
    - Create a colour chart to show the colours of this emotion.
    - Find a story that talks about this emotion.
    - Write a label for this emotion and colour it in the emotional colours.

KS2/3

1. Show the children a range of pictures of people expressing emotions.

2. Ask them to describe the emotions – furrowed brow, down-turned mouth, eyebrows pointing inwards towards the nose – Angry.

3. Divide the group into groups of 4–6 and put different pictures of people experiencing different emotions on the table.

4. Ask the children to put the coloured felt pens/crayons that go with each emotion on each emotion.

5. Share the colour ranges the children have come up with and discuss why they chose them.

6. Discuss the shapes that might go with different emotions.

7. Read *Michael Rosen's Sad Book* and look at the colours and pictures.

8. Ask the children to create a piece of art work, or a model using modelling clay, that shows an emotion.

9. Use the Emotions dice to create a small group story together. Sitting in a group, ask one child to roll the dice. Use the emotion shown to start the story, e.g. Happy – I was walking across the fields in the sunshine with my dog Patch, who was wagging his tail. He was very happy. The second person rolls the dice. Use the emotion shown to add to the story, e.g.

Frightened – All of a sudden a huge snarling dog ran out of the bushes towards Patch. He became very frightened. Continue the story around the group.

KS3

1. Share a range of pictures of people experiencing a range of emotions – discuss how they make our body feel.

2. Play Emotional Charades – choose one activity and one emotion and then act out that activity in that way of feeling to your group for them to guess e.g. hanging out the washing in an angry way.

3. Ask the young people to make a game that helps younger children understand different emotions.

4. Discuss the criteria together and agree.

5. Share the games with each other.

RESOURCES

1. Pens for flip chart
2. Sticky notes
3. Paper and pens
4. Coloured pens
5. Card
6. Emotions picture cards
7. Art work depicting emotions
8. Emotional story books for younger children
9. Emotional Charades cards
10. Emotions dice
11. *Michael Rosen's Sad Book*

IMPORTANT POINTS

- Emotions are a healthy part of life.
- All emotions are acceptable, however not all behaviours are acceptable.
- Emotions affect the whole body.

LEARNING LINKS

Speaking and listening, collaboration, information processing, questioning, observation, creativity, planning and organisation, teamwork.

REFLECTION

Questions:

Positive comment from child:

Positive comment from adult:

LEARNING DIMENSIONS		SOCIAL & EMOTIONAL SKILLS	
Strategic awareness		Emotional literacy	
Learning relationships		Neuroscience	
Curiosity		Self-regulation	
Creativity		Self-development	
Meaning making			
Changing & learning			
Resilience			

Frustrated	Sad
Frightened	Cross
Worried	Mad
Anxious	Tired
Jealous	Happy
Amused	Bored
Confused	Calm
Irritated	Panic
Hanging out the washing	Washing up
Sweeping the floor	Mowing the grass
Making the bed	Having a shower
Peeling potatoes	Ironing
Putting away your clothes	Reading a book
Cutting the hedge	Washing the car
Digging the garden	Painting the wall
Making dinner	Waiting for the bus
Sitting in detention	Waiting in the canteen
Painting	Doing your homework

Recognising and understanding emotions

SESSION OBJECTIVES

To understand feelings and emotions more fully and understand that they only last for moments in time and are not forever.

SESSION OUTCOMES

✓ To use a metaphorical weather map to describe feelings and emotions.

✓ To be able to imagine how somebody else is feeling.

LESSON PLAN

➢ To support children, remember the times when their class baby and parent showed a range of emotions or a story which the parent shared that talked about how the baby felt about something.

For those classrooms not able to undertake the Circles for Learning Project, video clips or photographs can be used to support the discussion around the topic and stimulate thoughts and ideas from the children and young people.

Task

KS1/2: To use a metaphorical weather map to describe feelings and emotions.

1. Show the children a range of emotions on Emotions cards. Name the emotions and think about what might have happened to have caused them to feel that way.

2. Use a range of questions to help the children understand that emotions do not last forever. Share the 90-second rule found by Dr Jill Bolte Taylor. She found that the chemicals released by the body that create the emotions we feel only last in our body for 90 seconds.

If we can learn to 'ride the wave of emotions' and not get caught up in the cognitive – thinking about them – then they will pass.

3. Talk about when they have felt some strong emotions and get them to think how they could show this as a weather map. Happy – bright sunny day with blue sky. Sad – grey rainy day.
4. Some children will use what may seem like strange weather to describe things – ask them to explain and share their reason.
5. For some children 'Happy' can be a rainy day because they have a happy memory associated with rainy days.
6. Help the children to celebrate difference and understand that it can add to the richness of what we do.
7. Share the weather map sheet with the children and get them to fill this in.
8. Share the pictures at the end and discuss what they have done together.
9. Ask the question, What have you learnt that you didn't know before this lesson?

RESOURCES

1. Large flip chart
2. Pens for flip chart
3. Sticky notes
4. Paper and pens
5. Weather map activity sheet
6. Emotions cards [SEAL: Photocards of Feelings: https://www.tes.com/teaching-resource/seal-photocards-of-feelings-primary-6095733]
7. Different types of weather pictures

IMPORTANT POINTS

- Feelings and emotions do not last forever.
- We can share how we feel by describing feelings as an internal weather map.

LEARNING LINKS

Speaking and listening, collaboration, information processing, questioning, observation, creativity, planning and organisation, teamwork.

REFLECTION

Questions:

Positive comment from child:

Positive comment from adult:

LEARNING DIMENSIONS		SOCIAL & EMOTIONAL SKILLS	
Strategic awareness		Emotional literacy	(green)
Learning relationships		Neuroscience	
Curiosity		Self-regulation	
Creativity		Self-development	(green)
Meaning making	(orange)		
Changing & learning	(orange)		
Resilience			

My internal weather map	Feeling	Weather map
How do you feel today?		

Understanding facial expressions

SESSION OBJECTIVES

To interpret facial expressions.

SESSION OUTCOMES

- ✓ Recognise happy, sad, angry, worried, frightened and excited facial expressions.
- ✓ Understand the 'shades of meaning' within emotions.
- ✓ A poem reflecting emotions.
- ✓ A musical composition.

LESSON PLAN

- ➢ Ask the children to think about a time when their class baby or their parent experienced an emotion.
- ➢ Discuss what that was about – what had led up to it and how the parent had soothed the baby.

For those classrooms not able to undertake the Circles for Learning Project, video clips or photographs can be used to support the discussion around the topic and stimulate thoughts and ideas from the children and young people.

Task

KS2/3: To create a poem to describe an emotion.

1. Show the children a face and ask what the emotion is.
2. Can they think of synonyms for this emotion?

3. Divide the class into groups/tables and give each group a face reflecting an emotion – children carousel around to fill in metaphors on faces:

   As sad as a rainy day, as happy as sunshine at the beach etc.

4. Ask the children to choose a face to create a poem on.

Sadness is

- (smell) Soil drenched with rainwater
- (sight) A tiny, empty chair
- (touch) An open paper-cut sliced through soft skin
- (hear) Howl of a caged hound
- (taste) Semolina on a hot day
- (colour and/or object) Steel barbed wire surrounding a scarlet flower

Alternatively create musical sounds to accompany an emotion. This could be through computer software, adding voices – 'Audacity' programme.

RESOURCES

1. Large flip chart
2. Pens for flip chart
3. Emotion faces
4. Poem exemplar

IMPORTANT POINTS

A baby can tell the difference between different faces at 3 months old.

LEARNING LINKS

Speaking and listening, information processing, social awareness, literacy.

REFLECTION

Questions:

Positive comment from child:

Positive comment from adult:

LEARNING DIMENSIONS		SOCIAL & EMOTIONAL SKILLS	
Strategic awareness		Emotional literacy	
Learning relationships		Neuroscience	
Curiosity		Self-regulation	
Creativity		Self-development	
Meaning making			
Changing & learning			
Resilience			

Happy

Sad

Worried

Angry

Frightened

is..........

(Smell)..

(Sight)..

(Touch)..

(Sound)..

(Taste)..

(Colour/Object)

....

Sadness is.........

(Smell) Soil drenched in rainwater

(Sight) A tiny empty chair

(Touch) An open paper cut sliced through soft skin

(Sound) The howl of a caged hound

(Taste) Semolina on a hot day

(Colour/Object)
Steel barbed wire surrounding a scarlet flower

Understanding body language

SESSION OBJECTIVES

To understand that the way we use our body shares how we may be feeling or experiencing a situation.

SESSION OUTCOMES

✓ To be able to say how a person is feeling from the way they are holding their body.

✓ To be able to use our body to communicate how we feel.

LESSON PLAN

➢ Ask the children to look at a range of pictures of their class mother and baby and to think about the shapes they both have in relation to the other.

➢ Ask the children to observe how the parent sits or stands in relation to their class baby.

For those classrooms not able to undertake the Circles for Learning Project, video clips or photographs can be used to support the discussion around the topic and stimulate thoughts and ideas from the children and young people.

Task

KS1: To play the body statue game.
KS2/3: To create a body sculpture that shows an emotion.
KS3: Active listening.

KS1

1. Using the words Happy, Sad, Frightened, Angry, Excited, write as many words as you can that mean the same.

   HAPPY: GLAD, CONTENT, LIGHT, GOOD, PLEASANT, CHEERFUL etc.

2. Use sticky notes to write the other words on and then place them under the chosen words.

3. Ask the children to make the faces of the words – describe the really good ones as to what you can see – upturned mouth teeth showing sparkly eyes.

4. Take photos as a resource bank.

5. Ask the children to stand up and show you a HAPPY body pose.

6. Explore the other poses – take photos of them as a resource bank.

7. Ask the children to move around the playground/hall and then when you call out an emotion to put their body into that emotional pose.

8. Ask the children to walk around the hall or playground and then greet each other in that emotional pose – ANGRY, SAD etc.

KS2/3

1. Put the words ANGRY, EXCITED, UNHAPPY, HAPPY, FRIGHTENED, CURIOUS, WORRIED on tables around the room.

2. Ask the young people to visit all the tables and write as many words as they can on sticky notes that mean the same/similar meanings to the word there.

3. Ask the young people to sit in groups at each table and put the words into order strongest to weakest:

   FURIOUS, ANGRY, CROSS, PEEVED, FED UP, TETCHY

4. Ask the young people to use the plastic bendy people to show the different emotions and photograph them.

5. Take one photo from each group and mix them up. Do a quiz – What do I feel?

6. Discuss the different photos and body postures.

KS3

1. Put the young people into groups.

2. Ask them to photograph each other showing a range of emotions.

3. Share the photos and discuss how our body can tell so much about how we are feeling.

4. Ask the young people to work in twos.

5. Let them choose one of the situation cards and then act out the situation in a thoughtful and considerate way demonstrating active listening, or in a thoughtless uninterested way showing poor active listening.

6. Role play for 2 min.
7. Discuss how this felt for the person talking.
8. Change the situation.
9. Choose one of the role plays to watch that was showing thoughtful, considerate, active listening.
10. Ask the young people to identify what was going on: eye contact, nodding of head, open body language, facing each other, rephrasing what they have said etc.

RESOURCES

1. Sticky notes
2. Paper and pens
3. Coloured pens
4. Plastic bendy people
5. Tablet or camera
6. Situation cards
7. Thoughtful and considerate cards
8. Facial expressions
9. Emotions cards [SEAL: Photocards of Feelings :https://www.tes.com/teaching-resource/seal-photocards-of-feelings-primary-6095733]

IMPORTANT POINTS

- We communicate more through body language than we do through words.
- Positive relationships depend on a good understanding of body language.

LEARNING LINKS

Speaking and listening, collaboration, information processing, questioning, observation, creativity, planning and organisation, teamwork.

REFLECTION

Questions:

Positive comment from child:

Positive comment from adult:

LEARNING DIMENSIONS		SOCIAL & EMOTIONAL SKILLS	
Strategic awareness		Emotional literacy	
Learning relationships		Neuroscience	
Curiosity		Self-regulation	
Creativity		Self-development	
Meaning making			
Changing & learning			
Resilience			

An interview for a part time job	Listening to a friend talk about their holiday
A date with your boyfriend/girlfriend	Your Mum explaining how to use the washing machine
A policeman giving you directions	A teacher explaining what you need to do for homework
A young child asking about a lost toy	A person who has lost their dog
Your Grandmother telling you about her trip to Bognor	Your Grandfather telling you about school when he was a lad
Your Dad explaining how to ride a bike	Taking an order in a cafe
Your Head of Year explaining about the exam you are about to take	The school secretary telling you about a phone call from your Mum

Kind, thoughtful listening with your full concentration and attention	Thoughtless, uninterested, distracted listening

Strong emotions: Angry

SESSION OBJECTIVES

To describe how to calm down after being angry.

SESSION OUTCOMES

- ✓ To understand that 'angry' can be experienced at different levels.
- ✓ To be able to use a variety of words to describe anger.
- ✓ To create an angry monster and describe how to calm it down.

LESSON PLAN

- ➢ Ask the children to recall a story that their class baby's parent has told them about their class baby getting angry or cross.
- ➢ Ask them why they thought the baby was angry and how their parent helped them manage.

For those classrooms not able to undertake the Circles for Learning Project, video clips or photographs can be used to support the discussion around the topic and stimulate thoughts and ideas from the children and young people.

Task

KS2: To create their own 'red beast'.
To create a list of angry words and place them on the thermometer.

1. Read *The Red Beast* by K.I. Al-Ghani.
2. Discuss this with the children.
3. Ask the children to draw and describe their red beast. They may wish to change the colour of their beast. If so, this is fine.

4. Discuss the angry thermometer and place angry words on it.

5. Discuss as a group how to get from one level to a calmer level and ask the children to describe the strategies they use.

6. Complete the How to Tame the Angry Monster Fact Sheet.

RESOURCES

1. Large flip chart

2. Pens for flip chart

3. *The Red Beast* by K.I. Al-Ghani

4. Angry Monster Fact Sheet

5. How to Tame the Angry Monster

6. Thermometer

7. Angry words

IMPORTANT POINTS

Anger is an emotion all people experience.

Strategies to help us calm down.

LEARNING LINKS

Speaking and listening, information processing, social awareness, literacy.

REFLECTION

Questions:

Positive comment from child:

Positive comment from adult:

LEARNING DIMENSIONS		SOCIAL & EMOTIONAL SKILLS	
Strategic awareness		Emotional literacy	
Learning relationships		Neuroscience	
Curiosity		Self-regulation	
Creativity		Self-development	
Meaning making			
Changing & learning			
Resilience			

Angry Monster Fact Sheet

Food

Habitat

Picture

Description

Characteristics

All about the Angry Monster

How to Tame the Angry Monster

Resources

Step One

Step Two

Step Three

Step Four

Strategies:

1.

2.

3.

Strategies:

1.

2.

3.

Strategies:

1.

2.

3.

Strategies:

1.

2.

3.

10
9
8
7
6
5
4
3
2
1

Angry

Cross

Tetchy

Irritable

Explosive

Rage

Furious

Irate

Seething

Infuriated

Incensed

Livid

Apoplectic

Murderous

Strong emotions: Sad

SESSION OBJECTIVES

To describe how to self-regulate after being sad.

SESSION OUTCOMES

✓ To understand that 'sad' can be experienced at different levels.

✓ To be able to use a variety of words to describe sadness.

✓ To create a sad picture and then show what could be used to self-regulate.

LESSON PLAN

➢ Ask the children to remember a time when their class baby become sad.

➢ Reflect on what caused this.

➢ Discuss how the parent managed this – what did they do? What was their tone of voice? What words did they use? How did they touch or hold the baby/toddler?

For those classrooms not able to undertake the Circles for Learning Project, video clips or photographs can be used to support the discussion around the topic and stimulate thoughts and ideas from the children and young people.

TASK

KS2: To draw a sad picture and show what might help someone lift their mood.

1. Share *Michael Rosen's Sad Book.*

2. Talk about the things that make us sad.

3. Think of as many words that mean sad as possible and then put them in order of most powerful to least powerful.

4. Ask the children to share what makes them feel better when they are sad.

5. Draw a picture showing something that has made them sad and then around the edge the things that cheer them up or make them feel better.

RESOURCES

1. Large flip chart

2. Pens for flip chart

3. *Michael Rosen's Sad Book*

4. Thermometer

5. Sad words

IMPORTANT POINTS

Sad is an emotion all people experience.

Strategies to help us self-regulate.

LEARNING LINKS

Speaking and listening, information processing, social awareness, literacy.

REFLECTION

Questions:

Positive comment from child:

Positive comment from adult:

LEARNING DIMENSIONS		SOCIAL & EMOTIONAL SKILLS	
Strategic awareness		Emotional literacy	
Learning relationships		Neuroscience	
Curiosity		Self-regulation	
Creativity		Self-development	
Meaning making			
Changing & learning			
Resilience			

Sad	Unhappy
Tearful	Upset
Heartbroken	Blue
Dejected	Despairing
Forlorn	Gloomy
Glum	Sombre
Woebegone	Down in the dumps
Weeping	Downcast
Grief-stricken	Out of sorts

How emotions impact on the way we behave

SESSION OBJECTIVES

To understand that emotions affect our behaviour and that we can choose how we respond to situations.

SESSION OUTCOMES

- ✓ To understand that emotions are like waves – they move on.
- ✓ A film strip showing causes and consequences.

LESSON PLAN

- ➢ Ask the children to remember a time when they observed their class baby showing an emotion.
- ➢ Discuss what they observed.
- ➢ Discuss what had caused the emotion or what had been the trigger.

For those classrooms not able to undertake the Circles for Learning Project, video clips or photographs can be used to support the discussion around the topic and stimulate thoughts and ideas from the children and young people.

Task

KS2: To show what happens to make someone feel an emotion, how their body feels and then how they regulate themselves.

KS3: To be able to create an image or model to show the run up to an emotion the emotion itself and then the aftermath.

KS2

1. Read *Wave* by Suzy Lee.
2. What emotions and feelings are portrayed in this book?
3. When do children think her amygdala (emotional alarm in the brain) kicked in – what was the response?
4. Look at the emotions film strip and discuss what may have happened before the picture.
5. Discuss what may happen after the picture.
6. What is it dependent upon – the thinking brain or the prefrontal cortex (PFC)?
7. Ask the children to choose a film strip and fill in what happens before and after.
8. Explore what we may want to do – behaviour affected by our emotions – amygdala hijacking our thinking brain and what we can choose to do.
9. Can children relate an example of when they have experienced this feeling? What did they do? What might they have done differently? Would this change the consequences?

KS3

1. Watch a video clip of a wave and link this to the feelings of an emotion.
2. Discuss the 90-second rule found by Dr Jill Bolte Taylor. She found that the chemicals released by the body that create the emotions we feel only last in our body for 90 seconds. If we can learn to 'ride the wave of emotions' and not get caught up in the cognitive – thinking about them – then they will pass.
3. Ask the young people to think of a time when they felt a strong emotion, draw it on the middle section of the film strip and then share what happened before and what happened after. If they would like to change the response then they can use another film strip to show the other ways they could have responded.
4. Share the stories and reflect on the amygdala and how it hijacks the brain.
5. Share strategies to manage this that some people use:
    - Mindfulness
    - Meditation
    - Breathing techniques
    - Distraction
    - Meditation on the soles of your feet

RESOURCES

1. Large flip chart
2. Pens for flip chart
3. *Wave* – story book
4. Emotions film strip
5. Blank film strip
6. Stop clock

IMPORTANT POINTS

Meditation and mindfulness distraction techniques can help in managing emotions.

The 90-second rule.

LEARNING LINKS

Speaking and listening, literacy, empathy, Science.

REFLECTION

Questions:

Positive comment from child:

Positive comment from adult:

LEARNING DIMENSIONS		SOCIAL & EMOTIONAL SKILLS	
Strategic awareness		Emotional literacy	
Learning relationships		Neuroscience	
Curiosity		Self-regulation	
Creativity		Self-development	
Meaning making			
Changing & learning			
Resilience			

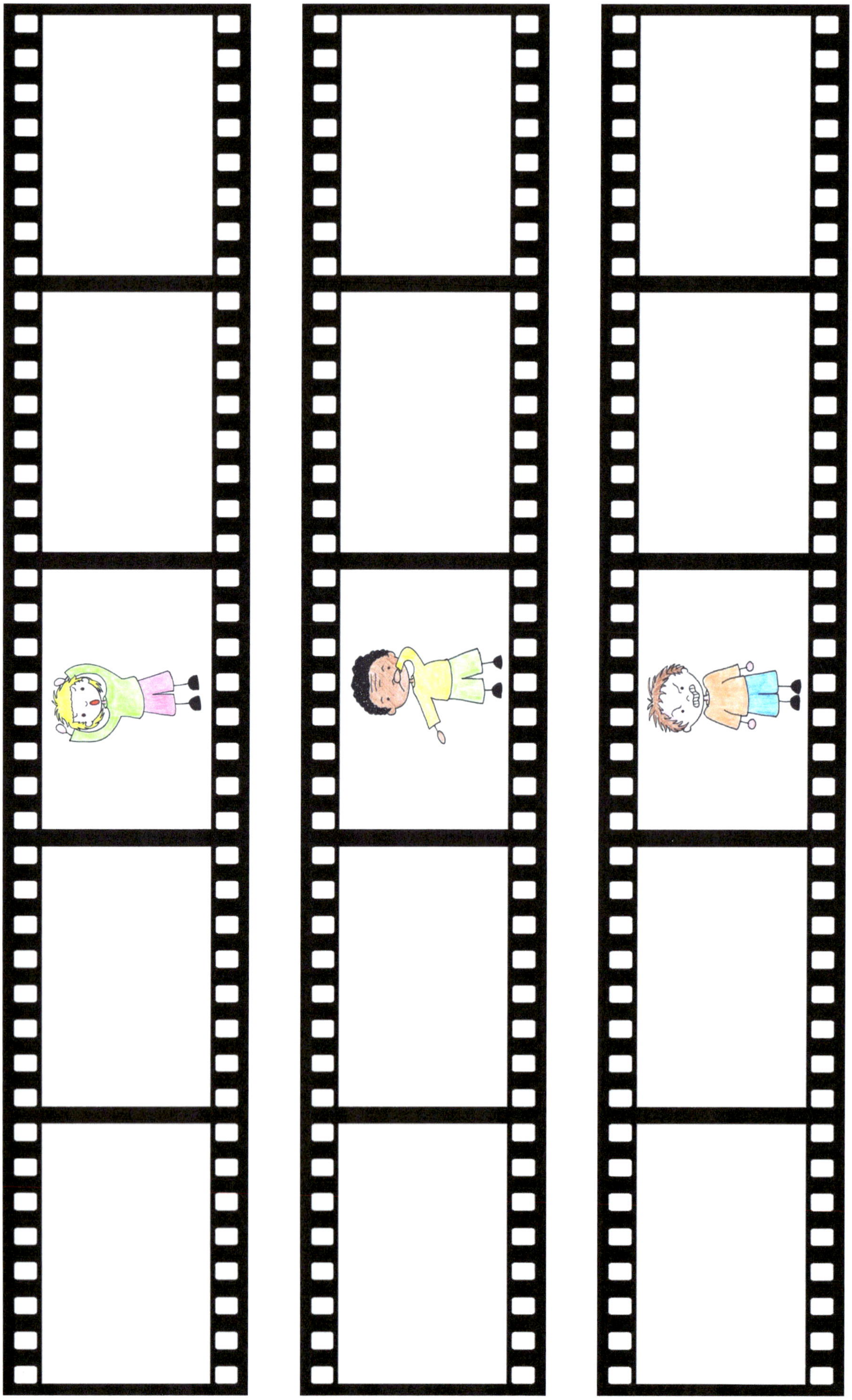

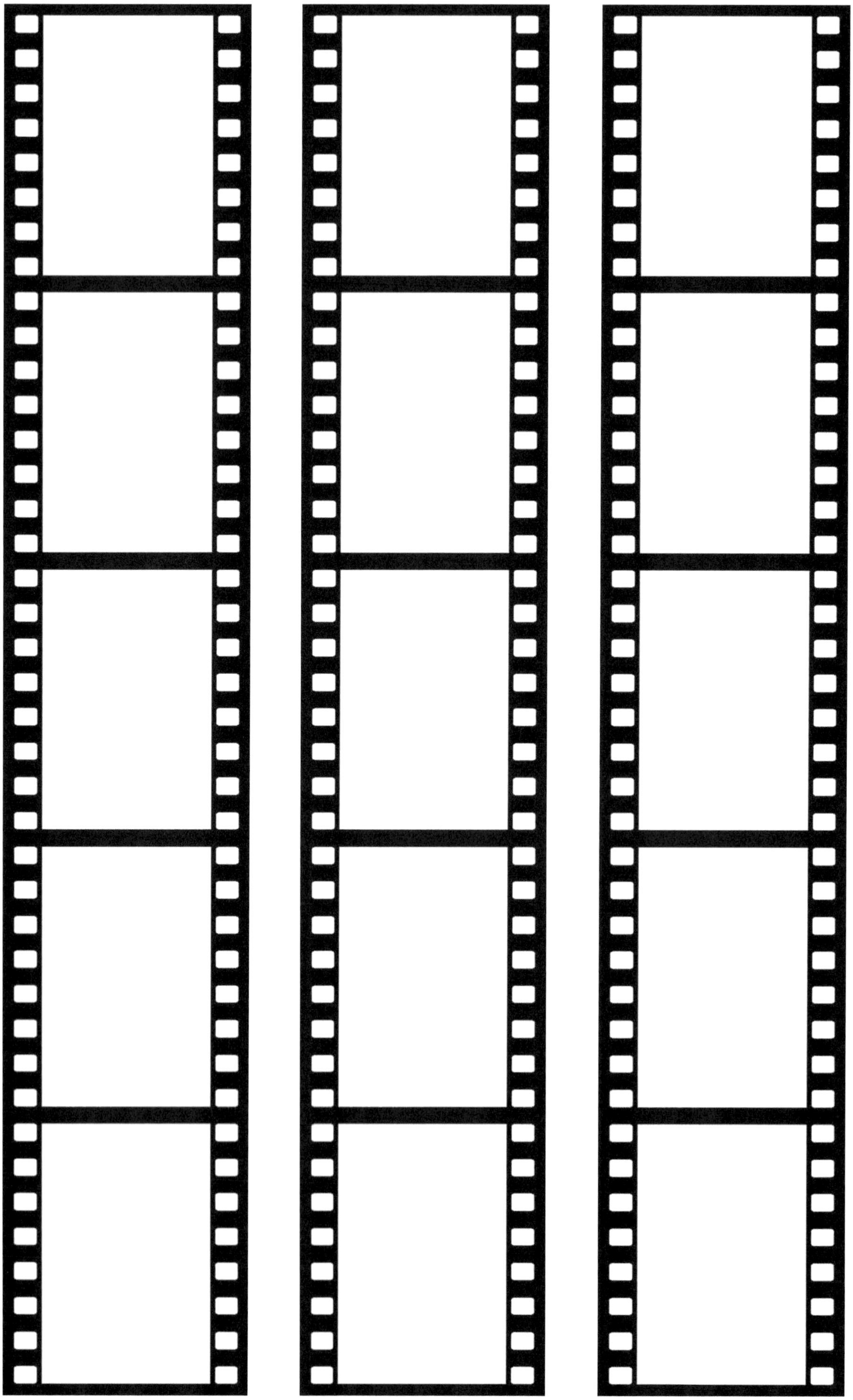

Chapter 2

Understanding emotions

There is only one person responsible for your happiness

1 2

SESSION OBJECTIVES

To explore the relationship between thoughts, feelings and behaviour.

SESSION OUTCOMES

✓ Poster displaying relationship between thoughts, feelings and behaviour.

LESSON PLAN

- Ask the children and young people to remember a time when they observed their class baby's parent noticing something the baby had done and commenting on it in a positive way.
- Discuss how that will have felt for the class baby.
- Discuss how the parent might see things after she has been up all night with the baby, who has had tummy ache or has been sick. Would she be as positive?

For those classrooms not able to undertake the Circles for Learning Project, video clips or photographs can be used to support the discussion around the topic and stimulate thoughts and ideas from the children and young people.

Task

KS1: To create a poster showing ways to be the 'Best I can Be.'

KS2: To create a poster: 'If you always do what you have always done you will always get what you have always got!'

KS1

1. Share the book *Why Am I Here?* by Matthew Kelly with the children.
2. Discuss and think about ways we can be the best we can be.
3. Ask the children to create a poster showing ways that they can be the best they can be.

KS2

1. Share the story about the artist Alison Lapper with the young people.
2. Discuss.
3. Ask them in pairs to think of 20 reasons not to do their homework. Then to think of 5 reasons not to make excuses.
4. In pairs ask the children to think of 3 things that are holding them back or preventing them from being successful or happy.
5. Working together, think of things that they could do to make a difference. Try to come up with 5 different strategies for each of the 3 things.
6. Together choose the one strategy that would make a difference.
7. Share the ones you would like with the other members of the class.

   EXAMPLE:
   No Money ⟶ Earn some by working or save more pocket money
   My Brother always picks on me ⟶ Act differently towards him.

8. Make a poster in pairs **'If you always do what you have always done then you will always get what you have always got.'**

RESOURCES

1. Sticky notes
2. Stuff Happens + You react = Outcome
3. Thoughts, Feelings, Actions Triangle
4. Large paper and felt tip pens
5. Lined paper
6. The book *Why Am I Here?* by Matthew Kelly

IMPORTANT POINTS

Understand the importance of thoughts feelings and behaviour and that there is only one person who is responsible for your happiness – **YOU**.

LEARNING LINKS

Self-awareness, emotional literacy, learning relationships, meaning making.

REFLECTION

Questions:

Positive comment from child:

Positive comment from adult:

LEARNING DIMENSIONS		SOCIAL & EMOTIONAL SKILLS	
Strategic awareness		Emotional literacy	
Learning relationships		Neuroscience	
Curiosity		Self-regulation	
Creativity		Self-development	
Meaning making			
Changing & learning			
Resilience			

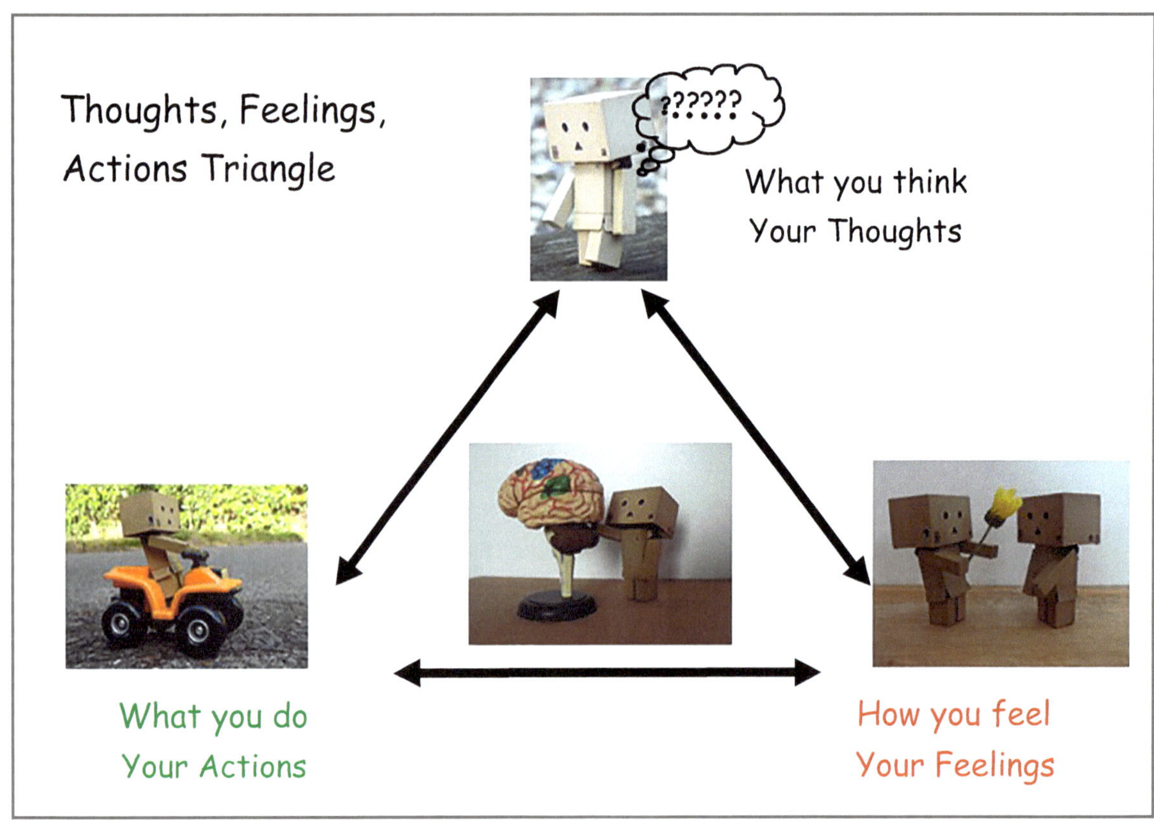

Magic Formula

Stuff happens + You react = Outcome

Coping strategies part 1: Making decisions

2 3

SESSION OBJECTIVES

To enable young people to discuss strategies they use when they need to make decisions.

SESSION OUTCOMES

✓ To enable young people to explore choices and the decision-making process.

LESSON PLAN

- Ask the children and young people to think about what they have learnt about being a parent from their class baby's parent. Is it more difficult than they thought?
- How do they think the parent feels when they face difficult decisions?

For those classrooms not able to undertake the Circles for Learning Project, video clips or photographs can be used to support the discussion around the topic and stimulate thoughts and ideas from the children and young people.

This is a follow-on lesson from Thoughts, Worries and Preoccupations in Chapter 3, 'Self-awareness'.

Pose the question, when faced with a difficult decision or dilemma, how do they feel?

Panic, confused, don't know what to do and so do nothing?

When we make no decision then that is our decision. This may be to avoid the uncomfortable feelings that decisions create, not wanting to get the decision wrong, allows us to blame somebody else when things go wrong.

It is important to be proactive with decisions rather than passive or reactive and not to be frightened or confused by the feelings that decisions can cause.

Task

KS2/3: To explore the decision-making process.

1. Ask the young people to think of a dilemma or decision they are trying to make. If they haven't really got one then get them make one up so that they can experience the process: What shall I have for tea? Where shall I go on holiday with my family? What shall I do at the weekend?

2. When you are faced with a decision or dilemma to solve, think of all the alternatives – however extreme these may be.

3. Put these alternatives on the crossroads sheet; if you need more sheets then use them.

4. Now travel down the various roads to the options you have chosen.

5. Draw or write what you find there, how you feel when you are there and what thoughts you have.

6. Imagine that you take a day visit to each place – write a postcard to your friend telling them about what you have experienced. If it helps score each place out of 10 for feelings, 10 for enjoyment and 10 for fulfilment.

The exercise could also be done by moving to 4 or so different places within a room and talking about what they experience in each place of opportunity OR by visualisation or mental imagery.

To do the exercise mentally, ask them to imagine going to each place of opportunity in turn. Ask them to talk in the present about what they find and how it feels:

I am now walking into my new college and it looks . . . I feel . . . .

Discuss the language of decisions:

I want to do it

I should do it

It will be good for me to do it

It is right for me

I'd better do it as other people want me to

I'd better do it as other people are counting on me to do it.

Which are the most powerful? Which ones do they find themselves using?

RESOURCES

1. Crossroads picture
2. Pens, pencils

IMPORTANT POINTS

- Decisions can be hard to make however strategies to help us can be useful.
- When we choose to not make a decision we are in fact making a decision.

LEARNING LINKS

Creativity, learning relationships, meaning making, emotional literacy.

REFLECTION

Questions:

Positive comment from child:

Positive comment from adult:

LEARNING DIMENSIONS		SOCIAL & EMOTIONAL SKILLS	
Strategic awareness		Emotional literacy	■
Learning relationships		Neuroscience	
Curiosity		Self-regulation	
Creativity		Self-development	■
Meaning making	■		
Changing & learning	■		
Resilience			

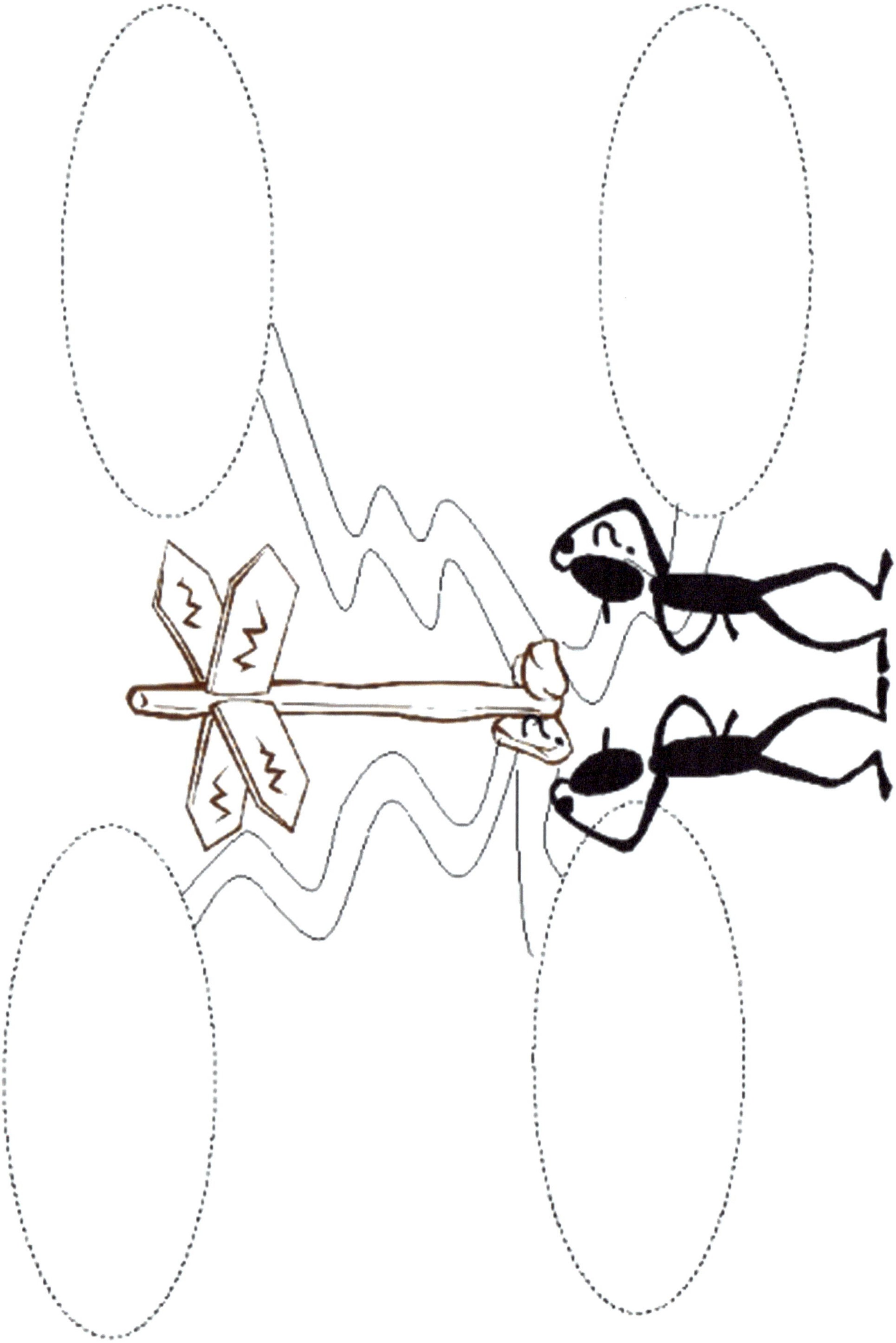

Coping strategies part 2: Managing anxiety

SESSION OBJECTIVES

To enable young people to explore how they manage when they feel worried or anxious in situations.

SESSION OUTCOMES

- ✓ To enable young people to identify how they adopt defensive behaviour when they feel worried or anxious.
- ✓ To enable young people to identify when other people are feeling defensive or anxious.

LESSON PLAN

- ➢ Ask the young people to remember what their class baby does when they feel unsure or anxious – they may reach for their parent, not leave their lap, suck their thumb or clutch their special blanket or toy.

For those classrooms not able to undertake the Circles for Learning Project, video clips or photographs can be used to support the discussion around the topic and stimulate thoughts and ideas from the children and young people.

Task

KS2: To make a list of questions that you could ask people when you join a new group as a way to make new friends.

KS3: To role play meeting new people.

KS2

1. Ask the young people how they deal with things – what are their coping strategies for meeting new people? Going to new places? Doing new things?

2. Introduce the concept of defence mechanisms – ways we defend ourselves when we don't like things – we can't climb onto Mum's lap anymore or suck our thumb so we find other ways of protecting ourselves from perceived danger. This is linked with being hurt or experiencing unpleasant feelings.

3. Discuss the many ways we look after ourselves: Don't go to new places, play on our phone, distract ourselves, use positive self-talk etc.

4. Working with a partner, write 6 questions that you could use when meeting someone new as a way to get to know them

5. Share these and then remind children of the work on body language, open or closed.

6. Role-play meeting someone and trying out your questions.

7. Discuss how it felt and how you knew if it was working for them. Introduce the work on Reciprocity.

KS3

1. Introduce the concept of defence mechanisms – ways we defend ourselves when we don't like things – we can't climb onto Mum's lap anymore or suck our thumb so we find other ways of protecting ourselves from perceived danger. This is linked with being hurt or experiencing unpleasant feelings.

2. Imagine you are going to meet a new group of people, do you:

   - Hide behind something – friend, book paper, phone, tablet
   - Protect yourself by building an imaginary wall around yourself – not talking to people or interacting
   - Use humour to hide behind – making jokes and clowning around.
   - Act in an over-excited and animated way where you lark and joke around
   - Become aggressive and full of I can . . . .
   - Behave like a person who knows everything – and so protect yourself that way hiding behind knowledge
   - Sit quietly and fade into the background hoping that you won't be noticed.
   - Manage the anxiety you are feeling and focus on the new friends you may make or on interacting with the people in the group.

3. Divide the group into smaller groups of 4. Ask each person to choose something in the room to hide behind that represents their defence system and then meet in their group and role play meeting each other for the first time, making small talk and chatting.

4. After a while people all drop their defences but remain in the group. If they wish they can pick up their defences at any time if they feel they need them.

5. Bring a halt to the exercise and ask the young people what they were feeling when they dropped their defences?

6. Ask the young people to watch for people's defences and notice how people protect themselves. When they do, ask them to try and work out what it is people are anxious about. Can they do anything to reduce their anxiety and make them feel better? What happens if they change their body language or use questions to engage them?

RESOURCES

1. Objects in the room

IMPORTANT POINTS

- It is important to understand that when we feel psychologically under threat we use defences to protect ourselves. This is because the amygdala has now been woken up and the alarm system is on.

- We can be aware of our defence mechanisms and control them.

- We can be aware of other people's defence mechanisms and try and put people at ease.

LEARNING LINKS

Creativity, learning relationships, meaning making, emotional literacy.

REFLECTION

Questions:

Positive comment from child:

Positive comment from adult:

LEARNING DIMENSIONS		SOCIAL & EMOTIONAL SKILLS	
Strategic awareness		Emotional literacy	
Learning relationships		Neuroscience	
Curiosity		Self-regulation	
Creativity		Self-development	
Meaning making			
Changing & learning			
Resilience			

Coping strategies part 3: Using positive memories

SESSION OBJECTIVES

To enable young people to understand that they have strategies and a self-support system to rely on when the going gets tough and it is up to them to make sure it is in good working order.

SESSION OUTCOMES

✓ To enable young people to use visualisation of the good memories they have to boost them when they feel down.

LESSON PLAN

- Ask the children and young people to think about the memories that their class baby is collecting each day and how they might influence his/her life.
- Ask the young people to think of some of the memories that their class baby's parent might be collecting about their child: first smile, first steps, crawling – all 'doing' memories.
- On their bed playing, in the bath blowing bubbles – all 'being' memories.

For those classrooms not able to undertake the Circles for Learning Project, video clips or photographs can be used to support the discussion around the topic and stimulate thoughts and ideas from the children and young people.

Task

KS2/KS3: Create a suitcase of uplifting memories.

1. Discuss the memories that the class baby is creating each day and how those memories and experiences influence them.

2. The baby has also got memories to call upon to support them. When they feel frustration they will know that they will be helped – because of all the times they felt that feeling and then were supported.

3. When they feel sad – they will know that comfort will come – because of all the times they have felt sad and then comfort comes.

4. We can all call on good memories to support us when we need them if we choose to.

5. Doing this is one of our self-support strategies.

6. We can choose what we think about. Some of our thoughts make us feel sad, angry or fed up – not such good thoughts. Others can lift our spirits, make us laugh, or feel happy. We have the choice of which ones we call up.

7. If you're waiting at the dentist, thinking of horrid times when you have hurt yourself or felt pain may not be the most sensible thing to do!!

8. When life gets tough it is often useful to remember our good memories, places we have been, friends we know and times that we have had fun and things have been good. This is why things like old fashioned photographs are so precious to older people or phones or social media are so important for young people – they hold our memories and have the ability to remind us and make us feel similar feelings.

9. Ask the young people to draw some of the good memories they might call upon around the suitcase. Share them with a partner and let them know the story behind them.

10. Ask each group to share a place they have been in their life which was utterly beautiful or amazing – a being memory. Get the young people to describe it in the present tense as though they are there describing what it is like and what they can see, hear, smell and feel. These are nourishing images or memories and can feed our soul.

RESOURCES

1. Suitcase of memories

2. Pens, pencils

3. Pictures of special places

IMPORTANT POINTS

- It is important to develop a range of strategies and self-support systems that you can use when you need them.

- Nourishing memories of places or times are good ways to feed the soul and make us feel better.

LEARNING LINKS

Creativity, learning relationships, meaning making, emotional literacy.

REFLECTION

Questions:

Positive comment from child:

Positive comment from adult:

LEARNING DIMENSIONS		SOCIAL & EMOTIONAL SKILLS	
Strategic awareness		Emotional literacy	■
Learning relationships		Neuroscience	
Curiosity		Self-regulation	
Creativity		Self-development	■
Meaning making	■		
Changing & learning	■		
Resilience			

Australia
PARIS
NEW YORK

Coping strategies part 4: We can do it!

2 3

SESSION OBJECTIVES

To enable young people to explore strategies to support them in making choices and being proactive in their life.

SESSION OUTCOMES

✓ To enable young people to share and discuss strategies to use when they need to make decisions.

LESSON PLAN

➢ Ask the children to focus on their class baby and a time when they persisted with a difficulty or problem – shape sorter or other such toy. Ask the children about the learning that was happening at the time. List the choices that the parent had.

1. Do the activity for the child.
2. Watch and wait for the child to ask for help.
3. Take the activity away, stating that the child can't do it and so isn't ready for this activity.
4. Show the child how to do the activity.
5. Watch and wait for the child to get upset and frustrated and then take the activity away.
6. Ignore the child and carry on with what they were doing.

For those classrooms not able to undertake the Circles for Learning Project, video clips or photographs can be used to support the discussion around the topic and stimulate thoughts and ideas from the children and young people.

Task

KS2/3: To explore decision-making strategies with each other.

1. Sometimes life can be confusing and we have to make choices. Sometimes life can feel like we are stuck, confused and have no idea how to get ourselves unstuck. Discuss how this feels and then ask for strategies people use to manage this.
2. It is important to help the young people see that they have the power to change things and that they do not have to stay stuck in the maze.
3. Ask the children and young people what strategy they use when they need to make a decision.
4. List them on the board and discuss the pros and cons of each.
5. Ask the children and young people to discuss what it feels like to be stuck and not know what to do.
6. What strategies do they use when they are stuck and don't know what to do?
7. Write them on the board and discuss the pros and cons for each.
8. Ask the questions – Do some people like being stuck? Help the young people think about why some people choose to stay stuck – they do not have to change their lives, confront difficult feelings or face fears, face the unknown.
9. Create a flow chart to show how they make a decision, including how they get themselves unstuck.

RESOURCES

1. Maze picture
2. Pens, pencils

IMPORTANT POINTS

- We have the power to make changes in our life.
- To make changes we may need to use a range of strategies to help us.

LEARNING LINKS

Creativity, learning relationships, meaning making, emotional literacy.

REFLECTION

Questions:

Positive comment from child:

Positive comment from adult:

LEARNING DIMENSIONS		SOCIAL & EMOTIONAL SKILLS	
Strategic awareness		Emotional literacy	
Learning relationships		Neuroscience	
Curiosity		Self-regulation	
Creativity		Self-development	
Meaning making			
Changing & learning			
Resilience			

Jelly babies: Looking after another

1 2

SESSION OBJECTIVES

To explore the responsibilities of being a care-giver.

SESSION OUTCOMES

- ✓ A diary/journal/health record of the jelly baby.
- ✓ A score chart.

LESSON PLAN

- ➢ Ask the children what they think it must be like to be a parent. Remind them of what they have observed with their class baby and their parent.

For those classrooms not able to undertake the Circles for Learning Project, video clips or photographs can be used to support the discussion around the topic and stimulate thoughts and ideas from the children and young people.

Task

KS1/KS2: To create a diary of how they looked after their jelly baby.

1. What have they seen their class parent do for their class baby?
2. What do they think makes a good parent? List the qualities they think a parent needs to be good.
3. Share with them that you are going to set them a challenge – they are going to be a parent for a week.
4. Give each child a jelly baby – and explain that it is theirs to care for and look after for a week.
5. Each morning the health visitor (classteacher) will give the jelly baby its 'check-up'. Points will be awarded each day. Criteria might include points for cleanliness, where and how they are kept . . . and in tact!!

6. A diary must be kept on how the jelly baby has spent its day and who with. It would be helpful if parents could join in and perhaps sign to say the children have kept their records accurately at home.

7. The jelly baby must be looked after at all times by the children or a jelly babysitter. Jelly babysitting must be paid with points collected (5 points an hour?)

8. At the end of the week, discuss the responsibilities that carers have when looking after children, elderly parents, etc.

9. What were the children's thoughts and experiences?

RESOURCES

1. Jelly babies

2. Record/diary

3. Score card

IMPORTANT POINTS

Care giving is a big responsibility

When you look after another you have to put your own needs and wishes on hold.

LEARNING LINKS

Emotional literacy, responsibility, self-awareness.

REFLECTION

Questions:

Positive comment from child:

Positive comment from adult:

LEARNING DIMENSIONS		SOCIAL & EMOTIONAL SKILLS	
Strategic awareness		Emotional literacy	
Learning relationships		Neuroscience	
Curiosity		Self-regulation	
Creativity		Self-development	
Meaning making			
Changing & learning			
Resilience			

NAME:							
JELLY BABY RECORD SHEET							
	Mon	Tue	Wed	Thur	Fri	Sat	Sun
Cleanliness							
Care							
Interaction							
Environment							
Stimulus							
Career							
Other							

NAME:							
JELLY BABY RECORD SHEET							
	Mon	Tue	Wed	Thur	Fri	Sat	Sun
Cleanliness							
Care							
Interaction							
Environment							
Stimulus							
Career							
Other							

NAME:							
JELLY BABY RECORD SHEET							
	Mon	Tue	Wed	Thur	Fri	Sat	Sun
Cleanliness							
Care							
Interaction							
Environment							
Stimulus							
Career							
Other							

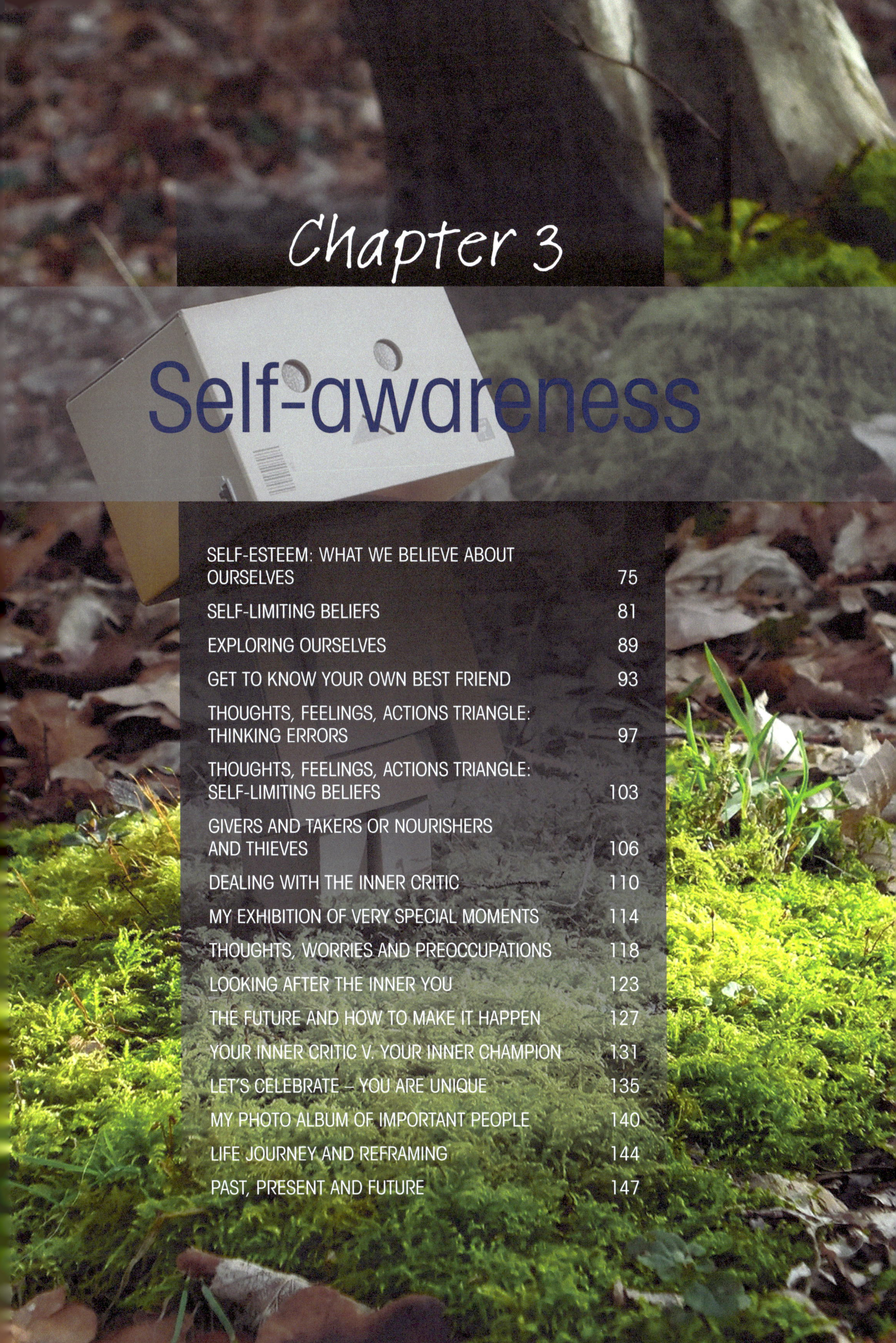

Chapter 3

Self-awareness

Self-esteem: What we believe about ourselves

SESSION OBJECTIVES

To develop a greater understanding of how we decide what to believe about ourselves.

SESSION OUTCOMES

- ✓ A range of labels that we have collected about ourselves.

LESSON PLAN

- ➢ Ask the children and young people to remember a time when their class baby's parent has given a label to the baby: 'She is so good at sleeping', 'He is such a fusspot'.

- ➢ Ask the children to think of labels that they have been given. Give examples of ones that you carry.

For those classrooms not able to undertake the Circles for Learning Project, video clips or photographs can be used to support the discussion around the topic and stimulate thoughts and ideas from the children and young people.

Task

KS1: Draw a picture of themselves with 6 labels they have been given.
Write 3 labels they would like to be given in the future.

KS2: To be able to list the labels that Maisy is given in the story.
To be able to write 6 labels that they have been given.
To create 4 labels they would like to achieve over the year ahead.

KS1

1. Remind the children of the labels that their class baby is collecting all the time.
2. Ask them to think of labels that they have been given. Write them on sticky notes. Choose yellow for ones they like and pink for ones they don't like.
3. Ask them to draw a picture of themselves and stick the labels around the picture.
4. Ask the children to write 3 labels they would like to collect in the future.
5. Share with each other what they need to do to collect them. Add these to their picture.

KS2

1. Share the story 'Maisy's Day' with the young people.
2. In pairs ask them to write on a sticky note all the labels she is given that day.
3. Divide the pile up into positive ones and negative ones.
4. Ask the young people to share a label that they have been given and let them explore what they think about it.
5. Demonstrate with Maisy's picture that the labels can be taken off if she doesn't want them.
6. Ask the young people to come up with 4 labels they would like to collect over the year ahead.
7. In pairs discuss what or how they can work to be given them.

RESOURCES

1. Large flip chart
2. Pens for flip chart
3. Sticky notes
4. Paper and pens
5. Coloured pens
6. Labels sheet
7. Sticky labels/ luggage tags
8. Maisy's story

IMPORTANT POINTS

- Self-esteem – what we believe is what we see.
- We have a choice over whether we take a label and how we behave.

LEARNING LINKS

Speaking and listening, collaboration, information processing, questioning, observation, creativity, planning and organisation, teamwork.

REFLECTION

Questions:

Positive comment from child:

Positive comment from adult:

LEARNING DIMENSIONS		SOCIAL & EMOTIONAL SKILLS	
Strategic awareness		Emotional literacy	
Learning relationships		Neuroscience	
Curiosity		Self-regulation	
Creativity		Self-development	
Meaning making			
Changing & learning			
Resilience			

MAISY'S DAY

The alarm went off and Maisy leapt out of bed. She needed to get a shower and wash her hair as she was going to audition for the school play. She got her things ready but her big sister was in the shower. She yelled for her to hurry up, telling her she needed to shower. Her Mum called up the stairs telling her to be quiet. 'You are always so loud Maisy; leave your sister to shower.'

Maisy tried to explain to her Mum why it was so important.

'If it was that important then you should have told your sister last night, really you are so disorganised.'

Maisy gathered up all her stuff but couldn't find her school bag. She called down to her Mum to see if she had seen it but Mum just told her to look for it where she had last left it!! 'Honestly Maisy, you really are forgetful.'

Finally her sister was out of the shower – quickly Maisy dashed in and slammed the door. She frantically got showered and washed her hair and then dashed back to her bedroom to dry it. Mum came into her bedroom and threw her towel at her. 'Maisy you are so untidy, please clean up after yourself. I'm fed up with doing it.'

Maisy quickly hung up her towel and then dashed downstairs for breakfast. Her little brother was struggling with the milk container lid. Maisy gave him a tickle and then helped him. He giggled and smiled at her. 'I love you Maisy,' he said as he gave her a cuddle. Mum looked up and smiled at Maisy.

'You know you really are good with your brother. Thank you.'

Maisy then grabbed all her things and dashed to the car. Her Dad was waiting to take her to school. She leapt in and then slammed the door. Dad frowned. He was not happy.

'Maisy I wish you would treat things with more respect. You really seem to have no idea about how to look after things.'

Maisy apologised and then sorted out her homework. Dad smiled. 'You know, when your Mum and I went to parents evening your Maths teacher was really pleased with your progress. He said you had been really working hard and that you were really focused in his class. Shame the Science teacher didn't think so, he said you often forgot your homework and were always talking to your friends. He said you were a really disruptive student. I can't understand how you can be so different.'

'I know Dad. I just really like the maths teacher, he really helps me.'

Maisy and her Dad finally got to school. 'Is it the auditions day today?' asked Dad.

'Yes,' said Maisy.

'I hope it goes well, you deserve it. You have worked really hard on learning your lines, you really do have a great memory and I know I am your Dad but I also think you have a lot of talent.'

'Thanks Dad, fingers crossed.'

Maisy jumped out of the car and went into school. As she walked in through the doors, her friends came to meet her and they all walked to their form room together. As they entered, Mr Smith the Deputy Head came in. He handed out the timetables for the auditions, Maisy was so excited to get one that she forgot to say thank you when he handed her the sheet.

'You know Maisy Turner, you really are one of the rudest students I know, not only don't you say please and thank you but I also saw you teasing one of the Year 7s the other day. I've got my eye on you so I suggest that you sort yourself out.'

'Yes Sir,' answered Maisy.

'What was all that about? asked her friend.

'I'm not sure. He seems to have it in for me, he's rather full of himself.'

Maisy grabbed the timetable and then set off for Maths, which was her first lesson. Mr Brown met her at the door. 'How's my grade A student doing? Did you manage the homework?'

Maisy nodded and smiled 'Yes Sir, I did, once I got going it was fine.'

'Well done Maisy. I really do think you have a brain for maths, you will go far.'

'Thanks Sir.'

Maisy finished Maths and then went off for the audition. She was really nervous and didn't see Mr Smith walk around the corner. She bumped into him and knocked his books flying. 'Oh God I am really sorry Sir, I wasn't concentrating I was trying to …'

'I don't want to hear your excuses young lady. You need to look where you're going. I am putting you in a lunchtime detention for running in the corridors. Perhaps that way you will learn that you are not the only person in this school.'

Maisy went to argue but then drew a deep breath and remembered the audition. Instead she smiled and said 'Yes Sir,' before turning and escaping into the drama room.

Self-limiting beliefs

SESSION OBJECTIVES

To develop a greater understanding about how our beliefs about ourselves impact on what we do and what we think we can do.

SESSION OUTCOMES

- ✓ To create a beliefs systems triangle poster.

LESSON PLAN

- ➢ Ask the children to think about the class baby. Ask them how the baby developed a picture of itself, what it can do what it can't do and how it feels about itself.
- ➢ Where did the evidence for its beliefs come from?

For those classrooms not able to undertake the Circles for Learning Project, video clips or photographs can be used to support the discussion around the topic and stimulate thoughts and ideas from the children and young people.

Task

KS1: To draw a picture to illustrate the elephant story.
KS2: To create a poster to show the beliefs systems triangle.

KS1

1. Ask the children to draw a picture of themselves and show all the things that they are able to do around it, i.e. draw, write, run, walk, skip etc.
2. Share the elephant story with the children.
3. Discuss what they think about the story.

4. How might the story relate to them?

5. Where do they get the idea that they are good or bad at something? What is their evidence? How can they change this?

6. Ask the children to draw the things they would like to be able to do in a year's time on their picture.

7. Ask the children to share their posters: What I can already do, What I want to be able to do next year, What I need to be able to achieve this.

KS2

1. Link this lesson to the previous one on labels and how these are given to us by other people as we grow and develop.

2. Remind the children and young people that self-esteem (SE) isn't fixed; it fluctuates during the day depending on what we are doing. This is because of our beliefs. If we think we are useless in maths then our SE at this point will be low. If we think we are great at English (someone has told us so) then our SE will be high and we will believe we can do it.

3. What we believe impacts on how we behave, act and do something.

4. Introduce the beliefs systems triangle poster.

5. Put up the 'A mind stretched to a new idea never returns to its original dimension' quote.

6. Tell the story of the elephant.

7. Ask the young people to make a poster to show the beliefs systems triangle. Discuss what the poster needs to show and agree the success criteria. These might include:

   - The link between beliefs, experiences and behaviour.
   - That we have a choice about how we want to think about something.
   - It must be eye catching so that people stop and look and read it.
   - It must get the message across that we have choices in what we believe about ourselves quickly.

8. Display all the posters and ask the young people to do a silent viewing. Ask them to write what they liked, enjoyed or found thought-provoking about the posters on sticky notes.

9. You could also choose to make smaller ones up for children to have in their books or as a bookmark.

RESOURCES

1. Large flip chart
2. Pens for flip chart
3. Sticky notes
4. Paper and pens
5. Coloured pens
6. Elephant story
7. Beliefs systems triangle
8. Mind-stretcher quote

IMPORTANT POINTS

- What we believe about ourselves influences how we behave and what we do.
- We have a choice as to whether we challenge our beliefs and behave in a different way.

LEARNING LINKS

Speaking and listening, collaboration, information processing, questioning, observation, creativity, planning and organisation, teamwork.

REFLECTION

Questions:

Positive comment from child:

Positive comment from adult:

LEARNING DIMENSIONS		SOCIAL & EMOTIONAL SKILLS	
Strategic awareness		Emotional literacy	
Learning relationships		Neuroscience	
Curiosity		Self-regulation	
Creativity		Self-development	
Meaning making			
Changing & learning			
Resilience			

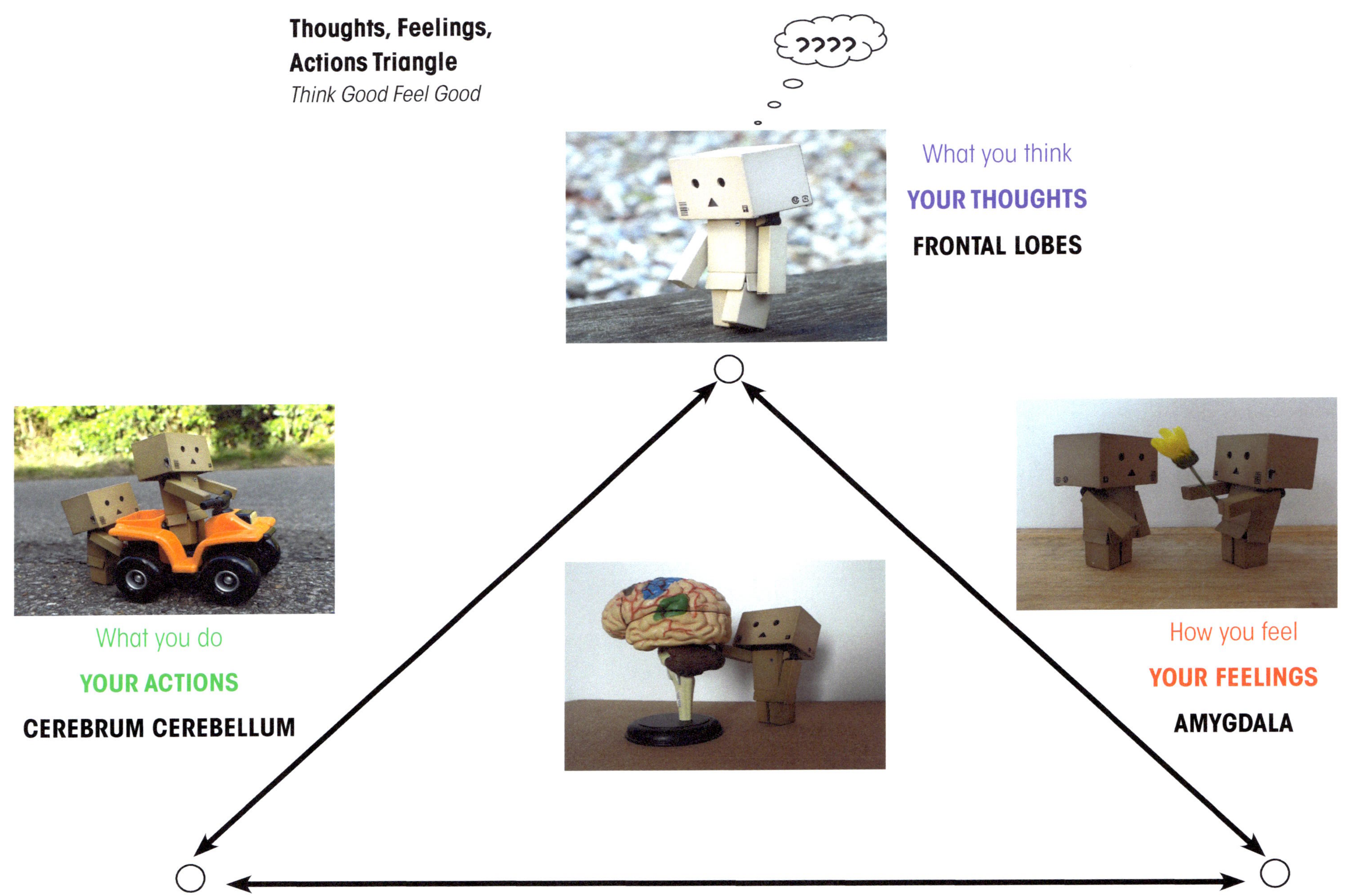
Thoughts, Feelings, Actions Triangle
Think Good Feel Good
????
What you think
YOUR THOUGHTS
FRONTAL LOBES
What you do
YOUR ACTIONS
CEREBRUM CEREBELLUM
How you feel
YOUR FEELINGS
AMYGDALA

THE ELEPHANT

What we believe about ourselves and the world actually creates the world we live in even if the belief is totally false.

Did you know that you can take a two tonne elephant, put a thin rope around its ankle and attach it to a small wooden peg in the ground and the elephant will not move?

The elephant could of course pull the stake out of the ground in an instant and go off wherever it wanted to and have a wonderful time. So why doesn't it?

When it was a baby elephant, a heavy chain was attached to its ankle and it was tied to a strong post in the ground. It learnt that every time it tried to get away it couldn't and if it kept trying it hurt its ankle. Consequently it grew up with the belief 'If you put a tie around my ankle then I cannot move.' A totally false belief in this instance. In fact elephants have been known to die in fires tethered in this fashion because they believed they could not move.

Fleas have been shown to do a similar thing. A flea can jump 18 cm upwards from the table which given the fact that it is only 2.5mm long is quite amazing. It would be the same as us jumping over a 30 storey building. However if a flea grows up in a jar it learns to only jump the height of the jar – or it hits its head. If you then take the lid off the jar the flea will still only jump to the height it has learnt is safe – which means it doesn't escape.

This is exactly what your BELIEFS are like – both the good ones and the not so helpful ones. They are like a rope around your ankle keeping you from doing things in your life.

The Beliefs Systems Triangle

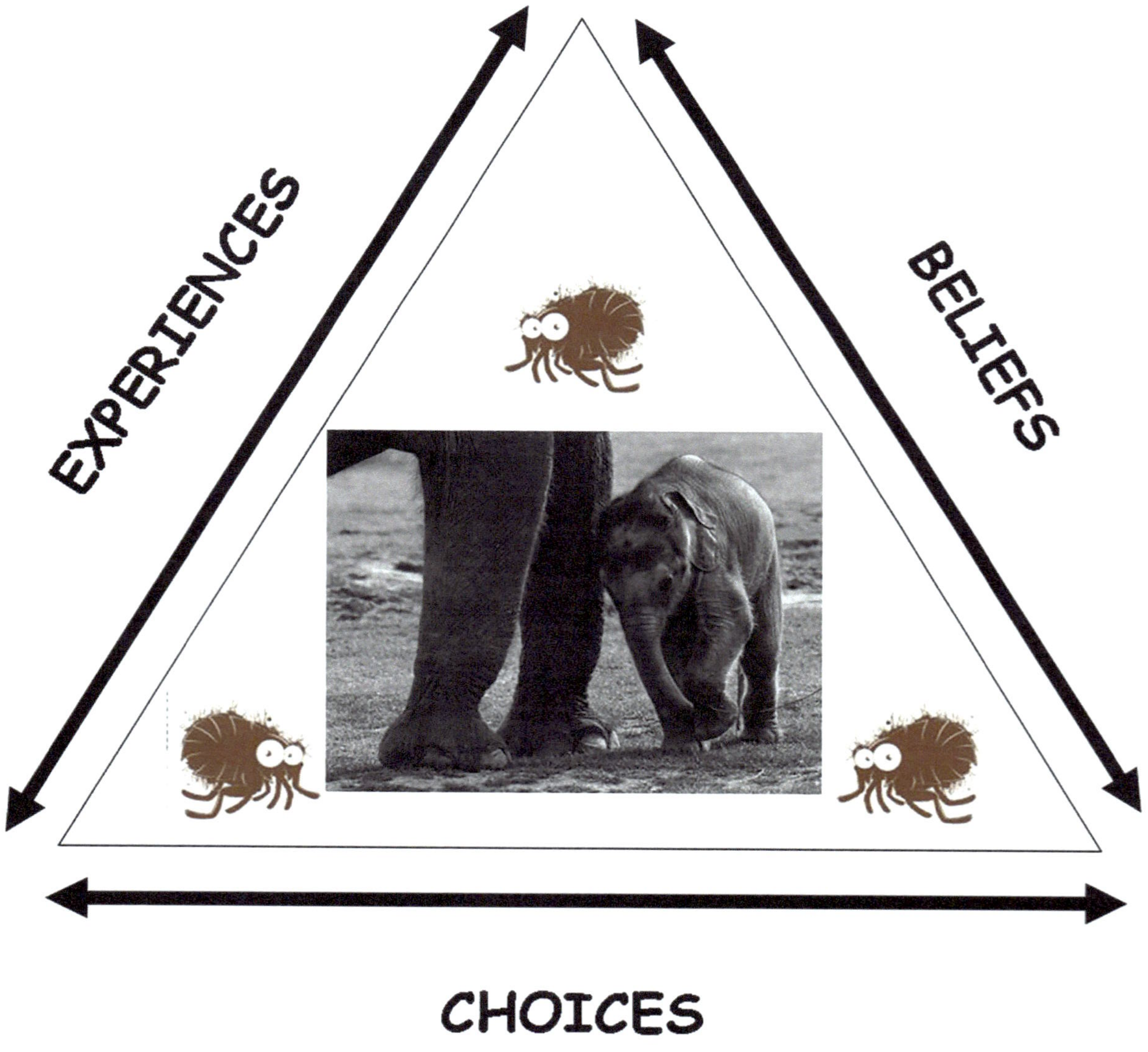

BELIEFS

CHOICES

EXPERIENCES

Exploring ourselves

SESSION OBJECTIVES

To understand that we are made up of true or core beliefs in ourselves and also of false parts.

SESSION OUTCOMES

✓ To understand more about ourselves and what we are like.

LESSON PLAN

➢ Ask the young people to describe their class baby, what they are like, what they enjoy, what they dislike etc.

For those classrooms not able to undertake the Circles for Learning Project, video clips or photographs can be used to support the discussion around the topic and stimulate thoughts and ideas from the children and young people.

Task

KS2/KS3: To identify qualities and traits that they have which make them who they are.

1. When the children and young people describe the class baby, write their description on a sticky note and attach sticky notes with what they say onto a picture of the baby. Remind the children about the work on labels.

2. Sometimes we need/want to fit in with a group and so we take on parts that the group believes.

3. On the drawing of the jigsaw head ask the young people to write their thoughts feelings, qualities and traits that they think are important in making up who they are e.g. love for X, kindness, intelligence, good at art, dancer.

4. Ask them to colour in pieces that they are not really comfortable with – parts that are not really them.

5. Think of aspects of yourself that you are denying – that have not been OK to be, think or feel, e.g. enjoy classical music, think that God exists or that violence is wrong. It may have been that these things were not acceptable within your family. Draw or write them on the pieces at the side of the picture.

6. It is useful if the facilitator can share something about themselves that is different from their partner or their family.

7. Celebrate who you are.

8. Ask if anyone has a story to share when they felt very much themselves or a time when they felt that what they were presenting was not their true self but a false self.

9. Share the 'Success' rainbow poem by Barbara Smallwood and Steve Kilborn.

RESOURCES

1. Head and jigsaw picture

2. Pens, pencils

3. Sticky notes and picture of their class baby

4. 'Success' rainbow poem, http://www.dyslexia.tv/freethinkersu/wisdom_success_smallwood.htm

IMPORTANT POINTS

- We are made up of many special qualities, traits, thoughts and ideas.

- We can change aspects of our self if we feel safe and supported.

LEARNING LINKS

Creativity, learning relationships, meaning making, emotional literacy.

REFLECTION

Questions:

Positive comment from child:

Positive comment from adult:

LEARNING DIMENSIONS		SOCIAL & EMOTIONAL SKILLS	
Strategic awareness		Emotional literacy	
Learning relationships		Neuroscience	
Curiosity		Self-regulation	
Creativity		Self-development	
Meaning making			
Changing & learning			
Resilience			

Get to know your own best friend

SESSION OBJECTIVES

To explore the Thoughts, Feelings, Actions Triangle.

SESSION OUTCOMES

- ✓ Understand the Thoughts, Feelings, Actions Triangle and the impact it can have.
- ✓ A Friendship Wheel with positive comments about their best friend – themself!

LESSON PLAN

- ➢ Ask the children and young people to describe their class baby.
- ➢ Ask them to remember how the parent describes their baby.

For those classrooms not able to undertake the Circles for Learning Project, video clips or photographs can be used to support the discussion around the topic and stimulate thoughts and ideas from the children and young people.

Task

KS2/3: To create a list of things about their best friend – themselves!

1. Give each child an envelope with their name on it and explain inside is their best friend.
2. Ask them all to open up the envelope and see if you have got it correct.
3. Suggest that if we do not like or love ourselves how can we expect anyone else to. Remind the children and young people about the Thoughts, Feelings, Actions Triangle. Help them to

make the link between what we think about ourselves and how we behave and how we then feel.

4. Ask them to use the Friendship Wheel and fill it in for themselves.

5. Pair up the children and ask them to add comments onto their Friendship Wheels. Remind the children and young people that this needs to be positively done.

6. Ask the children to write on a postcard/speech bubble sticky notes a positive thing to say to their best friend each day as they look in the mirror.

RESOURCES

1. Sticky notes

2. Friendship Wheel

3. Mirrors – enough for one each and placed inside an envelope.

4. Thoughts, Feelings, Actions Triangle

5. Post cards/speech bubble sticky notes

IMPORTANT POINTS

When we learn to care for ourselves as a best friend would we can celebrate who we are.

LEARNING LINKS

Self-esteem, self-awareness, emotional literacy.

REFLECTION

Questions:

Positive comment from child:

Positive comment from adult:

LEARNING DIMENSIONS		SOCIAL & EMOTIONAL SKILLS	
Strategic awareness		Emotional literacy	
Learning relationships		Neuroscience	
Curiosity		Self-regulation	
Creativity		Self-development	
Meaning making			
Changing & learning			
Resilience			

Friendship Wheel

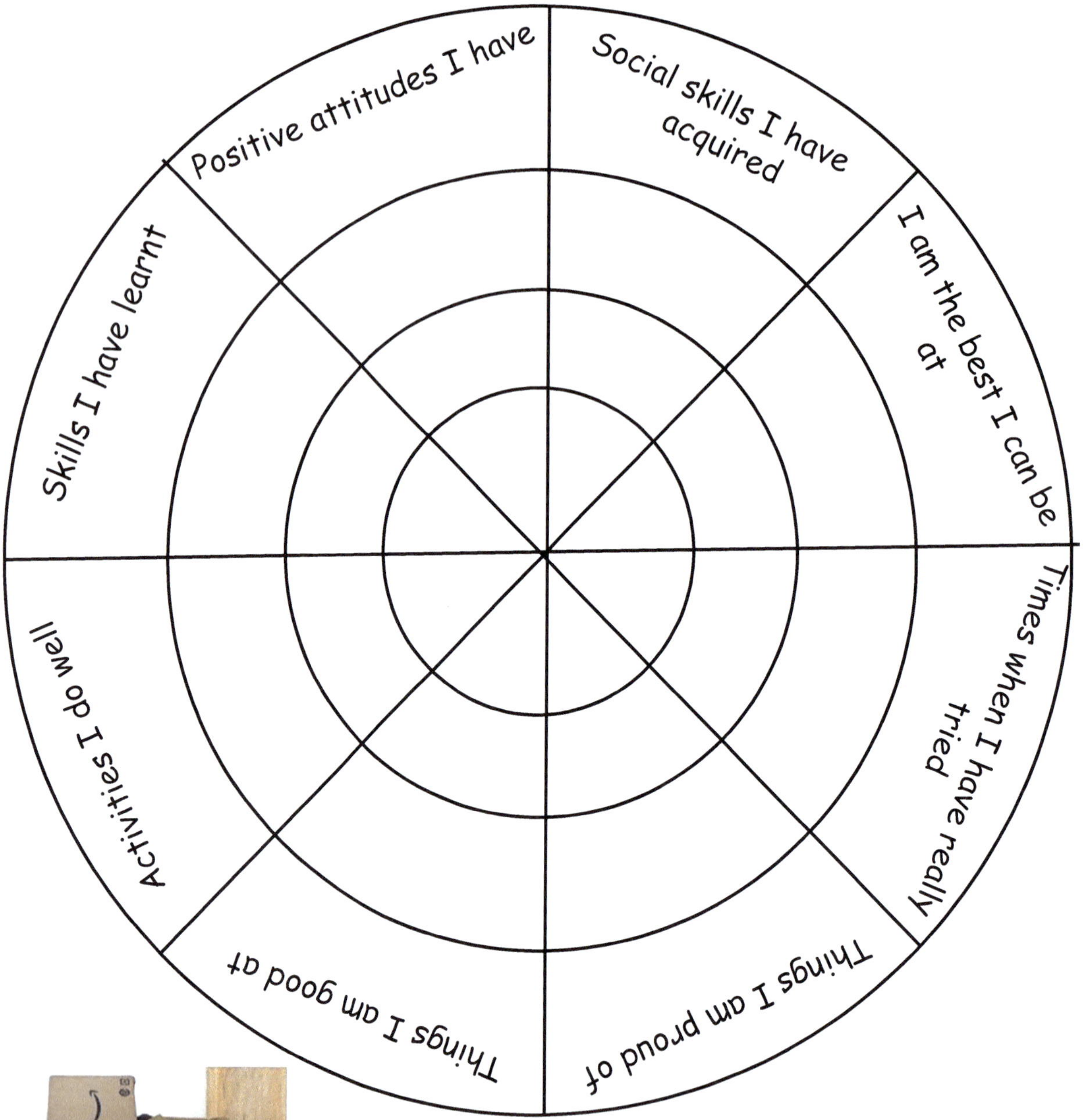

Positive attitudes I have

Social skills I have acquired

I am the best I can be at

Times when I have really tried

Things I am proud of

Things I am good at

Activities I do well

Skills I have learnt

Thoughts, Feelings, Actions Triangle: Thinking errors

SESSION OBJECTIVES

To understand how thinking errors can cause us to feel unpleasant and stop us from achieving what we want.

SESSION OUTCOMES

✓ A poster/advert for a magazine to demonstrate thinking errors that can impact on how we live our lives.

LESSON PLAN

➢ Ask the children and young people to think about a time when their class baby was really successful doing something. What sort of comments did their parent make to them?

➢ Ask the children and young people to think about a time when their class baby wasn't able to do something and got cross or frustrated. How did they know that was how they felt?

For those classrooms not able to undertake the Circles for Learning Project, video clips or photographs can be used to support the discussion around the topic and stimulate thoughts and ideas from the children and young people.

Task

KS2/3: To create a poster/advert for a magazine to show how our internal self-talk can affect what we do and how we do things.

1. Remind the children/young people about automatic thoughts and how they can be triggered by our beliefs.

2. Through a range of questions ask the children to describe the type of negative thoughts that they have experienced when things have gone wrong or are tough.

3. Share the 6 different categories with the children and ask them to make a poster/advert for a teen magazine to share these with other young people.

4. Discuss the success criteria for the poster together.

5. Once the posters have been made, ask the children to do a silent showing where they all walk around and look at the posters in silence.

6. Ask them to make a comment on a sticky note about why they like each poster that they have visited.

RESOURCES

1. Large flip chart
2. Pens for flip chart
3. Sticky notes
4. Paper and pens
5. Coloured pens
6. Thoughts, Feelings, Actions Flow Chart
7. The Magic Circle and Negative Trap activity sheet
8. Thinking errors definitions

IMPORTANT POINTS

- Our thoughts can be positive or can be negative and come from our early experiences which have created our beliefs.
- Our thinking errors can influence how we experience the world.

LEARNING LINKS

Speaking and listening, collaboration, information processing, questioning, observation, creativity, planning and organisation, teamwork, creativity.

REFLECTION

Questions:

Positive comment from child:

Positive comment from adult:

LEARNING DIMENSIONS		SOCIAL & EMOTIONAL SKILLS	
Strategic awareness		Emotional literacy	
Learning relationships		Neuroscience	
Curiosity		Self-regulation	
Creativity		Self-development	
Meaning making			
Changing & learning			
Resilience			

What were you doing?

What were you doing?

The

Magic Circle

Think about a time recently that you really enjoyed. Write or draw

How you felt

How you felt

What you were thinking

What you were thinking

The

Negative Trap

Think about one of your most difficult situations. Write or draw

Thoughts, Feelings, Actions Flow Chart

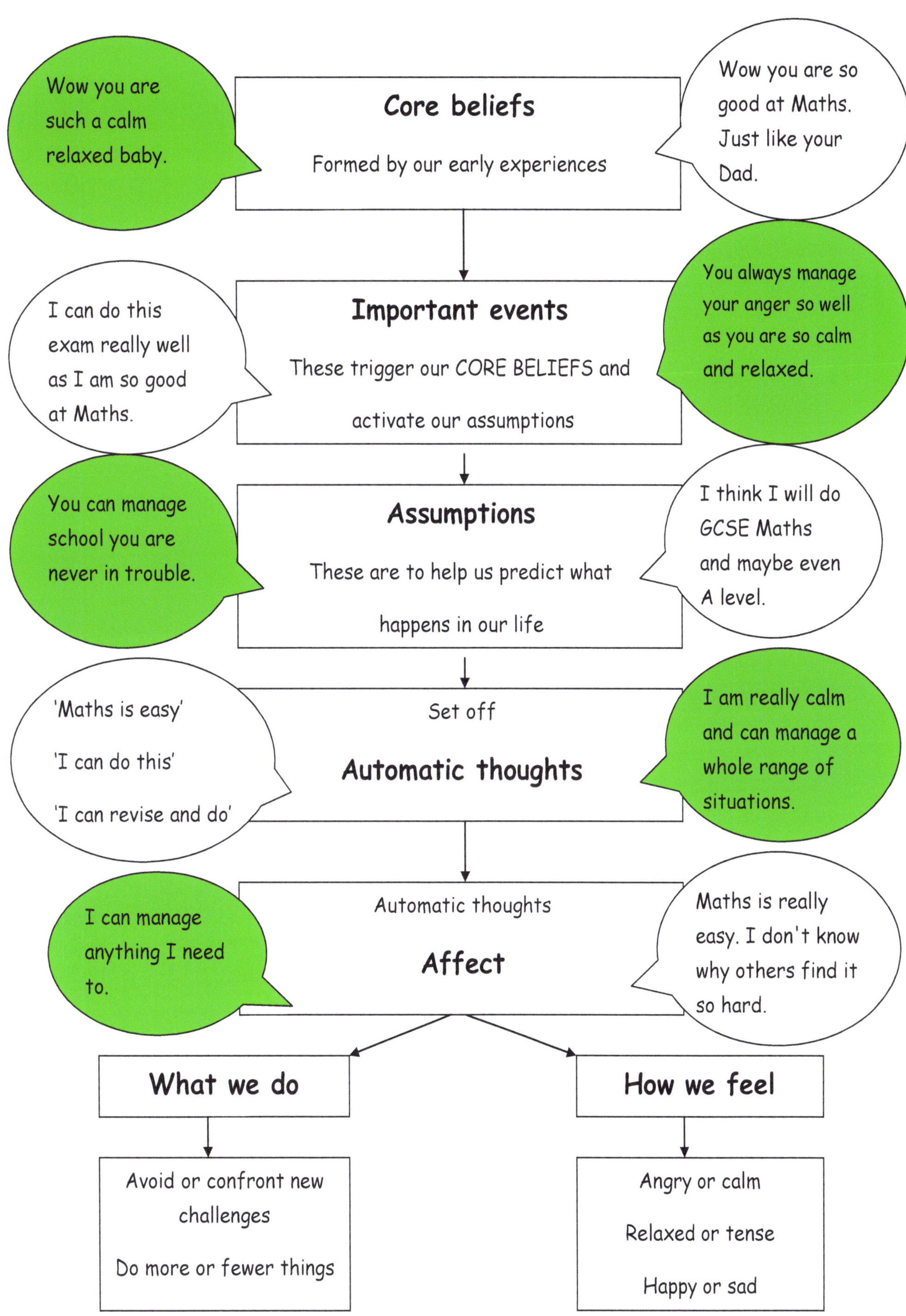

THINKING ERRORS OR DISTORTIONS

Thinking errors or distortions make us interpret events in a negative way. Positive events are not noticed or missed and are not accepted or given a positive understanding. This tends to mean that the negative events are the ones noticed and thought about.

Mental filtering is a thinking distortion where we filter things out of our conscious awareness. This is where we choose to focus on the negative things rather than on the positive things in a situation. For example – we choose to focus on what's not going well, mistakes we have made rather than the things that did go well or the achievements we made.

Jumping to conclusions is a thinking distortion where we make irrational assumptions about things. For example, we assume that something will happen in the future. This is called predicting or we assume that we know what someone else is thinking. These assumptions are not based on evidence or facts but are based on our personal feelings and opinions.

Personalisation is a thinking distortion that means we take the blame for everything that goes wrong with or in our life. If things don't work out well or as we hope we immediately blame ourselves. This is not based on any facts or evidence and is not related at all to whether we caused the situation.

Black and white thinking is a thinking distortion where we see things as either good or bad, right or wrong. This tends to mean we only see the extremes of the situation and are not able to recognise that there may be something in the middle or that a situation may have many shades of grey.

Catastrophising is a thinking distortion where we make everything much worse than it is. The problem or situation may be very small; however, if we get into the habit of catastrophising, we always make problems larger than life. This in turn then makes them truly difficult situations, events or circumstances to overcome.

Overgeneralisation is a thinking distortion where we make broad generalisations. These are often based on a single event from our past experiences which we then use as a basis for making assumptions. For example, whenever you say that 'Everyone always . . . My Mum never . . .', this becomes an overgeneralisation.

Labelling is a thinking distortion where we make global statements about ourselves or others based on behaviour we have experienced. These labels are based on past experiences or personal opinions and not on facts and evidence. For example 'You are a dreadful listener, you never remember anything,' 'You are really bad at maths, your test results are dreadful.'

Thoughts, Feelings, Actions Triangle: Self-limiting beliefs

SESSION OBJECTIVES

To understand how your early beliefs impact on your thoughts, feelings and actions.

SESSION OUTCOMES

✓ To develop a range of strategies to support them when the going gets tough, including how to challenge their own negative self-talk.

LESSON PLAN:

➢ Ask the children and young people to think of a time when their class baby heard something positive said about them.

For those classrooms not able to undertake the Circles for Learning Project, video clips or photographs can be used to support the discussion around the topic and stimulate thoughts and ideas from the children and young people.

Task

KS2/KS3: To explore self-talk and how to challenge this when it becomes negative.

1. Remind the children and young people about the work already undertaken on labels and beliefs.
2. Look at the Thoughts, Feelings, Actions Flow Chart and discuss. Ask them if they can identify a core belief that their class baby is taking on board.
3. What impact do they think this will have on their class baby's life in the future?
4. Ask the children if they are aware of a core belief of their own.

5. Ask the children to identify and share some of their automatic thoughts – good and bad.

6. With the use of questions encourage the children to explore what negative thoughts they get and how they make them feel. Pose the question are negative thoughts useful? Discuss when they are and when they are not. Record on the board.

7. Focus on when negative thoughts are not useful and ask what people do about them.

8. List the strategies they may include:
   Not listen, ignore, argue, switch off.

9. Other things that you could suggest is turn the volume down, change the voice – Donald Duck!! Thank your inner self for looking out for you and explain that these thoughts are not helpful at the moment.

10. Ask the children/young people to make a poster showing the different ways we can challenge our negative self-talk.

RESOURCES

1. Large flip chart
2. Pens for flip chart
3. Sticky notes
4. Paper and pens
5. Coloured pens
6. Thoughts, Feelings, Actions Flow Chart
7. The Magic Circle and Negative Trap activity sheet

IMPORTANT POINTS

- Our beliefs impact on what we do what we believe we can do and therefore on the way we experience the world.
- We can challenge our negative self-talk.

LEARNING LINKS

Speaking and listening, collaboration, information processing, questioning, observation, creativity, planning and organisation, teamwork.

REFLECTION

Questions:

Positive comment from child:

Positive comment from adult:

LEARNING DIMENSIONS		SOCIAL & EMOTIONAL SKILLS	
Strategic awareness		Emotional literacy	
Learning relationships		Neuroscience	
Curiosity		Self-regulation	
Creativity		Self-development	
Meaning making			
Changing & learning			
Resilience			

Givers and takers or nourishers and thieves

SESSION OBJECTIVES

To enable young people to understand that people in their life can nourish and nurture them (givers) or be unsupportive or stealers (takers).

SESSION OUTCOMES

- ✓ To enable young people to understand that some people in their lives are givers or nourishers and others are takers or stealers.
- ✓ To understand that they have the power to choose who they have in their life.
- ✓ To understand that they can choose whether they want to be givers or takers in other people's lives.

LESSON PLAN

- ➢ Ask the children and young people to think about how their class parent looks after their class baby. Share the sort of things the parent does for their child.

For those classrooms not able to undertake the Circles for Learning Project, video clips or photographs can be used to support the discussion around the topic and stimulate thoughts and ideas from the children and young people.

Task

KS2/3: To complete the givers and takers sheet.

1. Ask the children to think about what it is like to be the parent of their class baby. How much time and effort the baby takes up and how the parent is able to give as much as they do.

2. What do they think is the hardest thing that the parent does? Get up in the middle of the night, change nappies, get up early, help them when they cry....

3. Ask the young people to think of three people in their lives that give to them – nourish and nurture them.

4. Fill in the picture showing the people that nurture them and ask them to describe how they do this – love, support, time, encouragement etc.

5. Then ask them to fill in people in their life who take from them – what do they take and how does it make them feel – time, energy, fun etc.

TREAT THIS WITH SENSITIVITY

1. For some children this may be a parent who they care for, a brother or sister that they care for or a relative – what allows them to do this?

2. Now think of the people around you – are you a giver to them or a taker? If you feel that you are a taker from some people could you change this?

3. Do you feel that you have more to give? – How could you go about doing this? What things in school could you take part in that would support others?

RESOURCES

1. Givers or takers sheet

2. Pens, pencils

IMPORTANT POINTS

- It is important to understand some people nourish us and others take from us. We also nourish or take from others. We have choices that can be made.

LEARNING LINKS

Creativity, learning relationships, meaning making, emotional literacy.

REFLECTION

Questions:

Positive comment from child:

Positive comment from adult:

LEARNING DIMENSIONS		SOCIAL & EMOTIONAL SKILLS	
Strategic awareness		Emotional literacy	
Learning relationships		Neuroscience	
Curiosity		Self-regulation	
Creativity		Self-development	
Meaning making			
Changing & learning			
Resilience			

Nourishers

Thieves

Dealing with the inner critic

SESSION OBJECTIVES

To enable young people to discuss self-doubts, internal critical voices and negative beliefs they may have and to explore ways of challenging these.

SESSION OUTCOMES

- ✓ To enable young people to share and discuss self-doubts, internal critical voices and negative beliefs in themselves.
- ✓ To share and discuss strategies that can help challenge limiting beliefs.

LESSON PLAN

- ➢ Remind the children and young people of a time when they observed their class baby learn to do something.

  a) Remind the children and young people when their class baby wasn't able to do something.
  b) Ask them what they think the baby learnt about themselves on both occasions. What self-talk might they have been developing?
  c) Ask the children to focus on their class baby's parent. What do they think it must be like to be a parent? Do they think that parents always know what to do – is there a magical parenting school that they all go to? How do they decide what to do?

For those classrooms not able to undertake the Circles for Learning Project, video clips or photographs can be used to support the discussion around the topic and stimulate thoughts and ideas from the children and young people.

Task

KS2/KS3: To discuss self-doubts and negative beliefs and explore ways to challenge these. The aim of this lesson is to support young people verbalise self-doubts and negative beliefs they may have about themselves. By doing this they may also increase their understanding of how these may be self-sabotaging their own dreams and goals.

1. Ask the young people to think of their wishes, dreams and goals and to write these in the balloons without the pins to show that these dreams are really moving forwards. It is important to focus on these and to celebrate the small steps they have achieved each time they succeed.

2. Those dreams that they have which they feel they are blocking write on the balloons near the pins.

3. By the pin write what they think the block is – not brave enough, not skilled enough etc.

4. Get the young people to think about where this belief has come from – is it a label they were given – did they accept it without thinking?

   Example
   Balloon: I want to go to art school and design tattoos.
   Pin: You'll never make it you are not good enough.
   OR
   Balloon: I want to go to university and study psychology.
   Pin: No, you can't possibly do that, it is way too scary to go away from home where people love you and look after you, you're better off here.

5. Ask the young people to consider their self-limiting beliefs and to decide whether now is the time to get rid of them?

6. Share the Marianne Williamson poem 'Our Deepest Fear'.

7. Discuss with the young people how much 'being' is celebrated. Our society focuses on success by doing – getting a good job, a degree a house or a car. A 'being' success is living by certain human qualities – kindness, supporting people, inspiring people, bravery or making people laugh. What 'being' successes do they feel they would celebrate for each other?

RESOURCES

1. Balloons and pins

2. Pens, pencils

3. Marianne Williamson poem, 'Our Deepest Fear'

4. Sticky notes

IMPORTANT POINTS

- We are unique individuals with a range of very special qualities, traits and skills.
- We all have an inner critic that we have to learn to control and a champion that we need to create a louder voice for.

LEARNING LINKS

Creativity, learning relationships, meaning making, emotional literacy.

REFLECTION

Questions:

Positive comment from child:

Positive comment from adult:

LEARNING DIMENSIONS		SOCIAL & EMOTIONAL SKILLS	
Strategic awareness		Emotional literacy	
Learning relationships		Neuroscience	
Curiosity		Self-regulation	
Creativity		Self-development	
Meaning making			
Changing & learning			
Resilience			

My exhibition of very special moments

SESSION OBJECTIVES

To enable young people to celebrate what they have achieved.

SESSION OUTCOMES

✓ To be able to share things that they are proud of achieving.

LESSON PLAN:

- Ask the children and young people about their class parent and the memories that they might have of their baby.

- What sort of times do they think they may remember?
  First words, first steps – all 'doing' memories.
  They may also have memories of moments where they were just very happy watching or playing with their baby – 'being' memories stop.

For those classrooms not able to undertake the Circles for Learning Project, video clips or photographs can be used to support the discussion around the topic and stimulate thoughts and ideas from the children and young people.

Task

KS2/KS3: To celebrate and share some of our achievements.

1. Ask the young people to think of some of their own doing and being memories and draw or write them onto the sheet. Making their own exhibition of good moments.

2. Ask them to write around them the words or phrases that come to mind.

3. Ask them to choose music or songs to go with them.

4. Ask them to show another person around their exhibition and to talk them through it.

5. Ask the viewer to write down some of the words or phrases that they use when talking about the memories.

6. Ask the visitor to give the phrases that were used to the person whose exhibition it is at the end.

7. Share the stories they would like to share – try and ensure that you have both doing and being memories.

8. Share with the young people that the skill of gratitude is a very important one and that when practised it strengthens our attitudes and allows us to manage when things go wrong more easily.

The benefits of practising gratitude are nearly endless (see https://my.happify.com/hd/cultivate-an-attitude-of-gratitude/) People who regularly practice gratitude by taking time to notice and reflect upon the things they're thankful for experience more positive emotions, feel more alive, sleep better, express more compassion and kindness, and even have stronger immune systems. And gratitude doesn't need to be reserved only for momentous occasions: Sure, you might express gratitude after receiving a promotion at work, but you can also be thankful for something as simple as a delicious piece of pie. Research by UC Davis psychologist Robert Emmons, author of *Thanks!: How the New Science of Gratitude Can Make You Happier*, shows that simply keeping a gratitude journal – regularly writing brief reflections on moments for which we're thankful – can significantly increase well-being and life satisfaction (see https://greatergood.berkeley.edu/article/item/why_gratitude_is_good/).

RESOURCES

1. My exhibition poster A3 size

2. Pens, pencils

3. Sticky notes

IMPORTANT POINTS

- It is important to take time to remember and treasure special moments in our lives.

LEARNING LINKS

Creativity, learning relationships, meaning making, emotional literacy.

REFLECTION

Questions:

Positive comment from child:

Positive comment from adult:

LEARNING DIMENSIONS		SOCIAL & EMOTIONAL SKILLS	
Strategic awareness		Emotional literacy	
Learning relationships		Neuroscience	
Curiosity		Self-regulation	
Creativity		Self-development	
Meaning making			
Changing & learning			
Resilience			

MY MEMORIES

Thoughts, worries and preoccupations

SESSION OBJECTIVES

To understand that we have the power to influence our thinking.

SESSION OUTCOMES

✓ To explore our thoughts, worries and preoccupations.

✓ To understand that we can develop strategies to support us manage these.

LESSON PLAN

➢ Ask the young people to remember an observation where they watched their class baby thinking.

➢ Share what they saw and how they knew the baby was thinking.

For those classrooms not able to undertake the Circles for Learning Project, video clips or photographs can be used to support the discussion around the topic and stimulate thoughts and ideas from the children and young people.

Task

KS2/KS3: To understand that we have the power to influence what we think and therefore how we feel.

1. Watch 'What is a thought made of?', http://www.sciencealert.com/watch-what-is-a-thought-made-of
2. Discuss what the young people think about thinking!
3. Introduce and show the Mr Bean clip of the exam, https://www.youtube.com/watch?v=9LhLjpsstPY

4. Ask the young people to write down on the brain picture all the thoughts he might be having.

5. How is this affecting his logical cognitive thinking ability?

6. What happens when we worry? We tend to ruminate – the worry thought goes round and round our head and starts to take over.

7. Discuss strategies that they use when this happens. Are some people greater worriers than others? How does this happen?

8. Introduce the word 'anxiety' and share how some people cannot control their worrying/ anxious thoughts when they get out of control.

9. Make a bookmark of strategies to use when Worry Hits

10. Make a cartoon character from the Worry Hit Squad

11. Share what the children and young people have created.

RESOURCES

1. Head and brain picture

2. Upstairs and downstairs brain

3. Pens, pencils

4. Brain model

IMPORTANT POINTS

- We can develop strategies to support us keeping a positive way of thinking.

- Anxiety is when our flight or fight response has got out of control. Some people have anxiety disorders and need help managing these.

LEARNING LINKS

Creativity, learning relationships, meaning making, emotional literacy.

REFLECTION

Questions:

Positive comment from child:

Positive comment from adult:

LEARNING DIMENSIONS		SOCIAL & EMOTIONAL SKILLS	
Strategic awareness		Emotional literacy	
Learning relationships		Neuroscience	
Curiosity		Self-regulation	
Creativity		Self-development	
Meaning making			
Changing & learning			
Resilience			

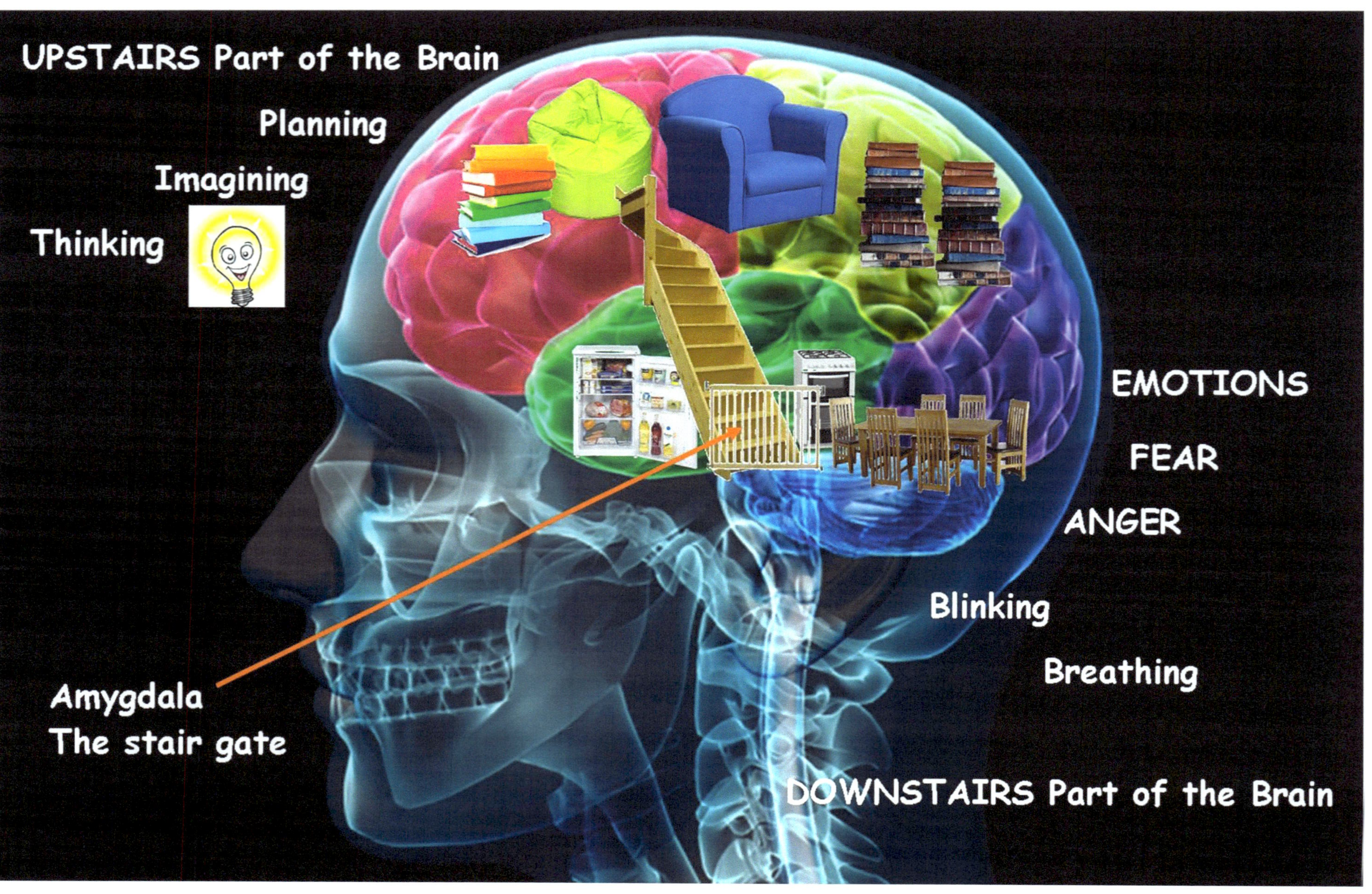
UPSTAIRS Part of the Brain
Planning
Imagining
Thinking
EMOTIONS
FEAR
ANGER
Blinking
Amygdala
The stair gate
Breathing
DOWNSTAIRS Part of the Brain

Looking after the inner you

SESSION OBJECTIVES

To enable young people to understand that their own best friend is themselves.

SESSION OUTCOMES

✓ To enable young people to explore looking after themselves psychologically.

LESSON PLAN

➢ Ask the young people how their class parent looks after their class baby: food, play, talking, teaching, comfort, support, safety etc. Point out that these come under 3 main categories – emotionally, physically and psychologically.

For those classrooms not able to undertake the Circles for Learning Project, video clips or photographs can be used to support the discussion around the topic and stimulate thoughts and ideas from the children and young people.

Task

KS2/KS3: To explore ways that we look after ourselves psychologically by strengthening our inner champion.

1. How do they look after themselves emotionally, physically and psychologically?
2. Share examples and then in small groups get the young people to brainstorm ways in which they do this.
3. Share together.
4. Focus on the psychological way that we support ourselves and think of our inner critic and our inner champion.

5. How can we strengthen our inner champion or our own best friend?

6. Working in groups, write down some of the inner champion phrases that we can develop and start to use that would be helpful and supportive. Think of what we would say and how we would talk to our friends.

7. Create an Inner Champion job description as a group.

RESOURCES

1. Paper

2. Pens and pencils

3. Inner Champion sheet

4. Examples of job descriptions

IMPORTANT POINTS

- We have the power to make changes in our life.

- We can strengthen our inner champion and make its voice louder.

LEARNING LINKS

Creativity, learning relationships, meaning making, emotional literacy.

REFLECTION

Questions:

Positive comment from child:

Positive comment from adult:

LEARNING DIMENSIONS		SOCIAL & EMOTIONAL SKILLS	
Strategic awareness		Emotional literacy	
Learning relationships		Neuroscience	
Curiosity		Self-regulation	
Creativity		Self-development	
Meaning making			
Changing & learning			
Resilience			

WANTED INNER CHAMPION

JOB DESCRIPTION

Job Description

- Job Title
- Summary Description
- Tasks and Responsibilities
- Minor Functions
- Supervisor
- Qualifications
- Skills Necessary
- Experience Desired
- Working Hours

The future and how to make it happen

SESSION OBJECTIVES

To enable young people to think about their future and what they want to achieve.

SESSION OUTCOMES

✓ To explore and share what we would like our futures to be like.

✓ To promote feelings of potency and that the young people can make their own future happen.

LESSON PLAN

➢ Remind the young people of one of the baby observations and ask them what the baby might think of themselves. How might they have come to that conclusion?

For those classrooms not able to undertake the Circles for Learning Project, video clips or photographs can be used to support the discussion around the topic and stimulate thoughts and ideas from the children and young people.

Task

KS2/KS3: To explore what we would like in our futures and how we can achieve our goals.

1. Remind the young people about the work they have done previously on labels.
2. Think about the labels their class baby has already acquired from parents, from them or have given themselves.
3. Ask them to share what they think their class baby's parents want for the baby.

4. Ask them to put their parents/career or special person in their lives hat on.

5. As that special person, write down what they would like for their future on the star sheet.

6. Now ask them to write down what they want for their future.

7. Share the idea that we **CAN** make our own Heaven and Hell on earth in the relationships we choose, the choices we make, and the way that we live. Discuss this as a group – link this to how we perceive ourselves as a result of the labels or perceptions we have taken from our experiences.

8. Share the 'Success' rainbow poem by Barbara Smallwood and Steve Kilborn.

RESOURCES

1. Large sheets of paper A3 or above

2. Pens, pencils

3. Modelling clay

4. 'Success' rainbow poem, http://www.dyslexia.tv/freethinkersu/wisdom_success_smallwood.htm

5. Star sheet

IMPORTANT POINTS

- How we interpret what has happened in our life is important to the way we think and behave. We can change the way we think and experience the world.

LEARNING LINKS

Creativity, learning relationships, meaning making, emotional literacy.

REFLECTION

Questions:

Positive comment from child:

Positive comment from adult:

LEARNING DIMENSIONS		SOCIAL & EMOTIONAL SKILLS	
Strategic awareness		Emotional literacy	
Learning relationships		Neuroscience	
Curiosity		Self-regulation	
Creativity		Self-development	
Meaning making			
Changing & learning			
Resilience			

What I want for my child in life

Your inner critic v. your inner champion

SESSION OBJECTIVES

To enable young people to explore strategies to support them in making choices and being proactive in their life.

SESSION OUTCOMES

✓ To enable young people to share and discuss strategies to use when they need to make decisions.

LESSON PLAN

- Remind the children of ways their class baby's parent has described their child – she is such fun, she is so good with jigsaws, she was talking really early. Listen to the things that their parent tells their child – 'You are so clever', 'Look at you, you are so beautiful'.

All these experiences are being soaked up by the child and are the foundations for their growing sense of self.

For those classrooms not able to undertake the Circles for Learning Project, video clips or photographs can be used to support the discussion around the topic and stimulate thoughts and ideas from the children and young people.

Task

KS2/KS3: To develop positive self-talk.

Psychologists have found that owing to a young child's undeveloped sense of self, verbal and non-verbal messages given to them can be as powerful as hypnosis.

Young children take in these messages without question – they swallow them whole. These 'labels' or 'beliefs' then become part of them and they use them as reference points for the rest of their experiences.

If a child believes they are unlucky then they will only register the aspects of their life that support this belief. They will not see the times when this is not true. All this may have come from a comment by a parent telling the child that they are 'So unlucky, nothing ever works for you.' This part, however, will be forgotten.

1. Remind the young people of the work on the inner critic and their inner champion.

2. Using the sheet, ask the young people to write the negative scripts that they use towards themselves each day. Their 'Inner Critic Voice'.

3. Pair up with a partner and read the inner critic comments. Ask the partner to give them a 'champion' reply.

4. Then in a different colour write this reply from their champion in response on the sheet.

   EXAMPLE:
   Critic: You are so stupid you can't get anything right.
   Champion: I may have got this wrong but I am learning each time.

5. Sometimes your inner critic can tell you something that is useful.

You don't do as much with your life as you could. You are so scared of everything that you never take a risk.

This has a message that might need to be listened to. Your inner champ might answer: 'What you say is true and I am often cross with myself for not having a go. Perhaps we could go and get some help – there is a teacher at school I think I could talk to. She might know how to help me feel less fearful.'

RESOURCES

1. Inner Critic v. Inner Champion

2. Pens, pencils

IMPORTANT POINTS

- We have the power to make changes in our life.

- We have to choose who to listen to – our inner critic or our inner champion.

LEARNING LINKS

Creativity, learning relationships, meaning making, emotional literacy.

REFLECTION

Questions:

Positive comment from child:

Positive comment from adult:

LEARNING DIMENSIONS		SOCIAL & EMOTIONAL SKILLS	
Strategic awareness		Emotional literacy	
Learning relationships		Neuroscience	
Curiosity		Self-regulation	
Creativity		Self-development	
Meaning making			
Changing & learning			
Resilience			

Inner Critic v. Inner Champion

Let's celebrate – you are unique

SESSION OBJECTIVES

To celebrate the skills, traits and qualities we possess.

SESSION OUTCOMES

- ✓ To enable young people to identify and celebrate the skills, traits and qualities that they possess.
- ✓ To challenge our inner critic and release our best friend.

LESSON PLAN

- ➢ Ask the children to remember ways that their class baby's parent has described them. List them together.

For those classrooms not able to undertake the Circles for Learning Project, video clips or photographs can be used to support the discussion around the topic and stimulate thoughts and ideas from the children and young people.

Task

KS2/KS3: To create a gallery of assets for each other, showing the things each child is good at, is valued for, or has a talent in.

Either undertake this exercise individually or in small groups of 6 young people. If working in groups then it would be important for the groups to know each other.

Groups

1. Sit in a group around a table.

2. Give each young person a gallery of assets sheet. Ask them to put one thing that they are good at, proud of or like about themselves in a picture frame.

3. Then pass the sheets to the next person in the group who must write something that they like, admire or think the person is good at in another frame. Continue until the frames have all been filled and then pass them back to the person who they belong to.

4. It is really important that before the young people start this exercise they understand that they write only positive things in the frames.

Individually

1. If working individually, ask the young people to fill in the frames for themselves.

2. As they fill the frames in for themselves their inner critic might pop up and try and stop them – 'Don't be arrogant', 'You don't do that as well as ....' Discuss this with the young people. We all have internal voices that either criticise or support us.

3. Get the children to draw a cartoon picture of their inner critic. Get them to write the phrases their critic often uses around the edge of the picture. Get them to think of ways that they could use to quieten their inner critic. Make these funny – tape his mouth up! Change his voice to Donald Duck! Make him lose his voice!

4. Now ask the children to draw their inner critic's opposition – their champion – and write phrases around the page that their champion could use.

OR

5. Make an Inner Critic Wanted poster

RESOURCES

1. Gallery of assets

2. Pens, pencils

3. Plane paper

4. Inner Critic Wanted poster

IMPORTANT POINTS

- We are a unique individual with a range of very special qualities, traits and skills.

- We all have an inner critic that we have to learn to control and a champion that we need to create a louder voice for.

LEARNING LINKS

Creativity, learning relationships, meaning making, emotional literacy.

REFLECTION

Questions:

Positive comment from child:

Positive comment from adult:

LEARNING DIMENSIONS		SOCIAL & EMOTIONAL SKILLS	
Strategic awareness		Emotional literacy	
Learning relationships		Neuroscience	
Curiosity		Self-regulation	
Creativity		Self-development	
Meaning making			
Changing & learning			
Resilience			

MY ASSETS

WANTED

INNER CRITIC

DESCRIPTION

$10,000 REWARD

My photo album of important people

SESSION OBJECTIVES

To enable young people to take the time to remember the important and influential people that they have met and who have contributed towards they way they are.

SESSION OUTCOMES

- ✓ To enable young people to remember the important people in their lives who have contributed to the way they are.
- ✓ We can choose how people can remember or think about us.

LESSON PLAN

- ➢ Ask the children to think about their class baby and a time when they felt that they were safe enough to explore and learn.

For those classrooms not able to undertake the Circles for Learning Project, video clips or photographs can be used to support the discussion around the topic and stimulate thoughts and ideas from the children and young people.

Task

KS2/KS3: To celebrate the important people in our lives.

1. To ask the young people to think about who has had the greatest impact on their class baby.

2. To think about the ways that their class baby has experienced different people.

3. Ask them to think about 6 people that they have met in their lives who have influenced the way they are, behave and interact with the world.

4. Draw them on the sheet and share how they have had an impact on them within a small group.

5. Around the edge of the picture draw the words of encouragement that they would use if they were here to do so.

6. Talk about the fact that often our mentors or supporters are not our parents but other people we have met along the way.

7. Think how they would like to be remembered by another young person in their life – what would they like that person to write around their picture about them?

RESOURCES

1. Picture album

2. Pens, pencils

IMPORTANT POINTS

- It is important to take time to reflect on the people that have influenced our lives and to imagine what they would say to us if they were here.

- We can choose how people think about us. This may be linked to how we interact with people or the environment around us.

LEARNING LINKS

Creativity, learning relationships, meaning making, emotional literacy.

REFLECTION

Questions:

Positive comment from child:

Positive comment from adult:

LEARNING DIMENSIONS		SOCIAL & EMOTIONAL SKILLS	
Strategic awareness		Emotional literacy	
Learning relationships		Neuroscience	
Curiosity		Self-regulation	
Creativity		Self-development	
Meaning making			
Changing & learning			
Resilience			

My photograph album of important people

Life journey and reframing

SESSION OBJECTIVES

To create a life journey showing how the young person sees or has experienced their life.

SESSION OUTCOMES

- ✓ To create a journey showing the young person's life.
- ✓ To share how the young person sees their life journey.
- ✓ To introduce the concept of reframing.

LESSON PLAN

- ➢ As a group, think of all the milestones their class baby has gone through. Draw this as a road journey showing the events as special pictures. These can be symbols – as on an OS map – that stand for things or small cartoon pictures.

For those classrooms not able to undertake the Circles for Learning Project, video clips or photographs can be used to support the discussion around the topic and stimulate thoughts and ideas from the children and young people.

Task

KS2/KS3: to create a life journey map.

1. Ask the children and young people to create their own life journey map showing the events that they remember from their life. They can do this in as creative a way as they wish. They can use symbols to show the emotions of the events, i.e. weather map symbols – rain representing sad and thunder clouds representing something that made them angry. Or they might like to use road signs, music or create a mixture.

2. The landscape they create around their journey is important and they may wish to stay with this when describing their journey. 'I drew a forest here as it was a time when life was dark and gloomy and I was wondering about feeling lost' or they may wish to talk about what the metaphor stood for. 'I have drawn this time as a huge tornado and storm because it was the time when Dad left home and there were lots of arguments and it was really horrible.'

3. Once they have drawn their journey they can make themselves out of modelling clay and then walk their friend along their life journey road sharing what is happening. Share as much as they want/feel comfortable with.

4. Explore with the young people that it is how we think of things that is important. This mindset is something that we can change if we work hard. Explain how to reframe thoughts and events.

Reframing is a psychological technique that consists of identifying and then disputing irrational or maladaptive thoughts. Reframing is a way of viewing and experiencing events, ideas, concepts and emotions to find more positive alternatives.

1. Get the children to think of reframes for life events for Harry Potter as a group:

   Death of parents
   Mean uncle
   Small bedroom under the stairs
   Losing his uncle
   The scar on his forehead
   Having no family who wanted him at Christmas

RESOURCES

1. Large sheets of paper A3 or above

2. Pens, pencils

3. Modelling clay

IMPORTANT POINTS

- How we see interpret what has happened in our life is important to the way we think.

LEARNING LINKS

Creativity, learning relationships, meaning making, emotional literacy.

REFLECTION

Questions:

Positive comment from child:

Positive comment from adult:

LEARNING DIMENSIONS		SOCIAL & EMOTIONAL SKILLS	
Strategic awareness		Emotional literacy	
Learning relationships		Neuroscience	
Curiosity		Self-regulation	
Creativity		Self-development	
Meaning making			
Changing & learning			
Resilience			

Past, present and future

SESSION OBJECTIVES

To enable young people to think about their past, present and future and to explore how they influence each other.

SESSION OUTCOMES

✓ To explore our past, present and future and see how they can influence each other.

✓ To promote feelings of potency and that the young people can make their own future happen.

LESSON PLAN

➢ Ask the children to think about their class baby observations and to share what sort of memories their class baby will have of the past. Help them link the thought of anything being possible for their class baby to themselves.

For those classrooms not able to undertake the Circles for Learning Project, video clips or photographs can be used to support the discussion around the topic and stimulate thoughts and ideas from the children and young people.

Task

KS2/KS3: To explore how our past and present can influence our future.

1. Hand out the window picture and ask them to draw in one pane of glass an important view of their past.

2. Then ask them to draw an important view of their present.

3. Ask them to sketch an important view that they hope for in the future.

4. In the last pane of glass ask them to sketch a view that they fear from the future.

5. What can they do to increase the probability that the future they want will come true and not the one that they fear?

RESOURCES

1. Window picture
2. Pens, pencils

IMPORTANT POINTS

- We are in charge of our future.

LEARNING LINKS

Creativity, learning relationships, meaning making, emotional literacy.

REFLECTION

Questions:

Positive comment from child:

Positive comment from adult:

LEARNING DIMENSIONS		SOCIAL & EMOTIONAL SKILLS	
Strategic awareness		Emotional literacy	
Learning relationships		Neuroscience	
Curiosity		Self-regulation	
Creativity		Self-development	
Meaning making			
Changing & learning			
Resilience			

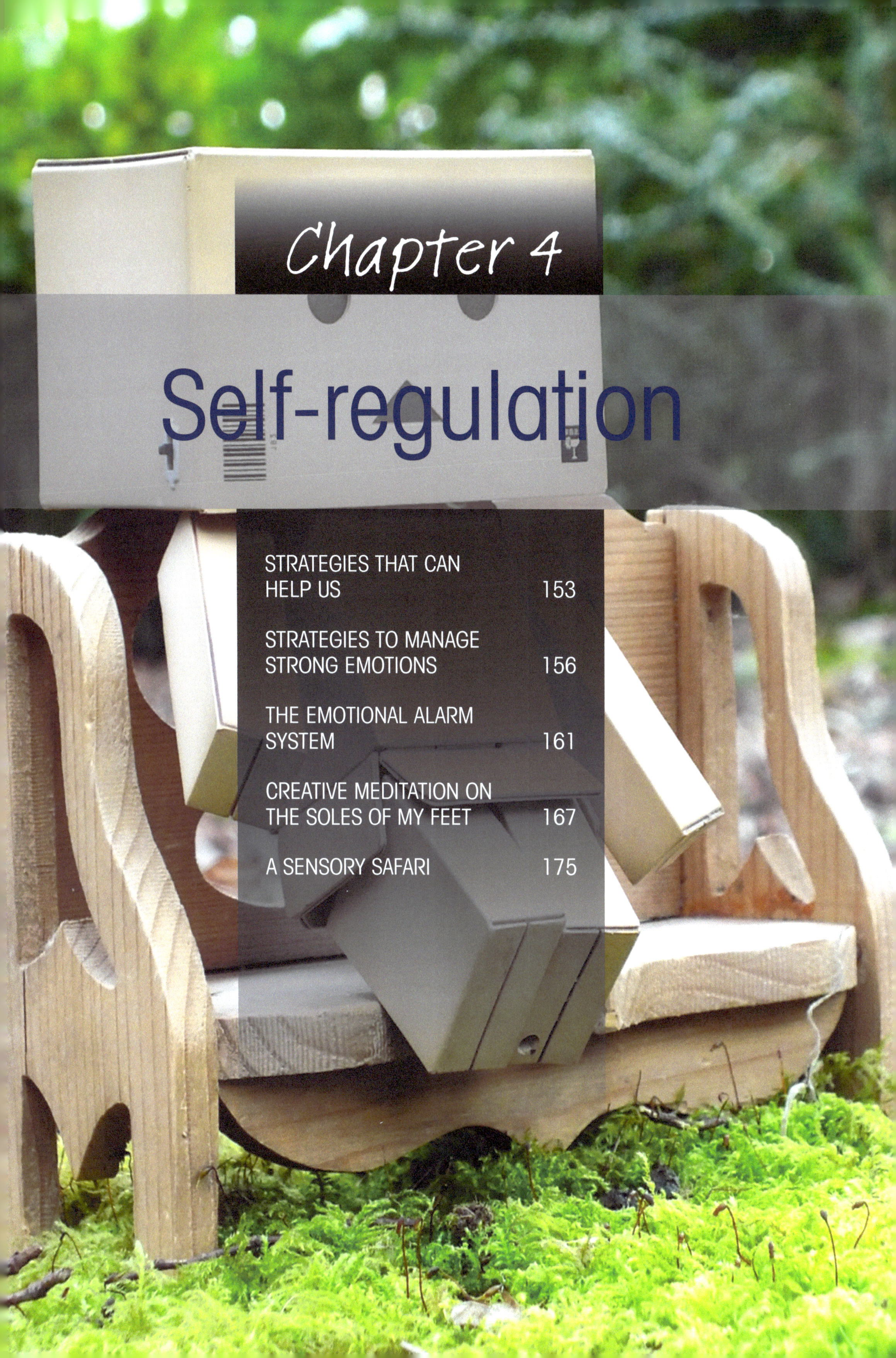

Chapter 4

Self-regulation

Strategies that can help us

SESSION OBJECTIVES

To identify things that help us manage our feelings.

SESSION OUTCOMES

- ✓ A list of examples of things that make people jealous.
- ✓ A range of strategies that help you when you experience jealousy.

LESSON PLAN

- ➢ Ask the children and young people what they think it is like having a baby brother or sister arrive in the family.

For those classrooms not able to undertake the Circles for Learning Project, video clips or photographs can be used to support the discussion around the topic and stimulate thoughts and ideas from the children and young people.

Task

KS2/3: To create a list of strategies to help them when they feel overwhelmed with emotions.

1. Read a story about jealousy.
2. Discuss times when they have felt this emotion and what it was like.
3. What does jealousy feel like? What does it look like?
4. Give children some examples of potential jealous situations – new baby arriving, new step family, new addition to established friendship group, brighter classmates. What are the negatives to these situations? Can they be turned to positives? Re-frame!

5. Give the children a small box and ask them to put strategies into it that make them feel better when they are finding feelings difficult to manage.

6. Share the strategies and discuss how they might work.

RESOURCES

1. Small slips of paper

2. Pens

3. Small box

4. Flip chart and pens

IMPORTANT POINTS

A baby can tell the difference between different faces at 3 months old.

Jealousy is a mixture of feelings, such as betrayal, hurt, envy, greed, inadequacy, fear, sadness, exclusion and loneliness. These feelings can be portrayed in many ways, some inappropriate.

LEARNING LINKS

Speaking and listening, literacy, self-awareness, empathy.

REFLECTION

Questions:

Positive comment from child:

Positive comment from adult:

LEARNING DIMENSIONS		SOCIAL & EMOTIONAL SKILLS	
Strategic awareness		Emotional literacy	
Learning relationships		Neuroscience	
Curiosity		Self-regulation	
Creativity		Self-development	
Meaning making			
Changing & learning			
Resilience			

Strategies to manage strong emotions

SESSION OBJECTIVES

To enable young people to understand that they have strategies and a self-support system to rely on when the going gets tough and it is up to them to make sure it is in good working order.

SESSION OUTCOMES

- ✓ To enable young people to recognise and improve their self-support system.

LESSON PLAN

- ➢ Ask the children to remember when their class baby struggled to cope with something and became upset or distressed. Share what 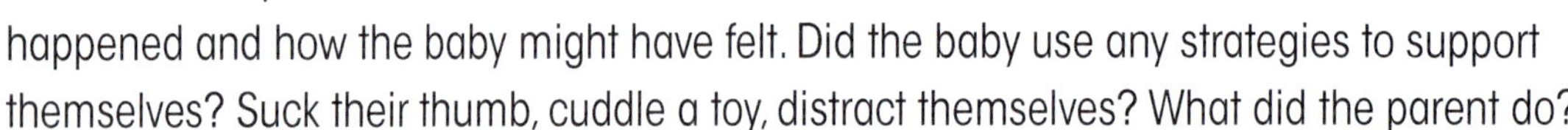
happened and how the baby might have felt. Did the baby use any strategies to support themselves? Suck their thumb, cuddle a toy, distract themselves? What did the parent do?

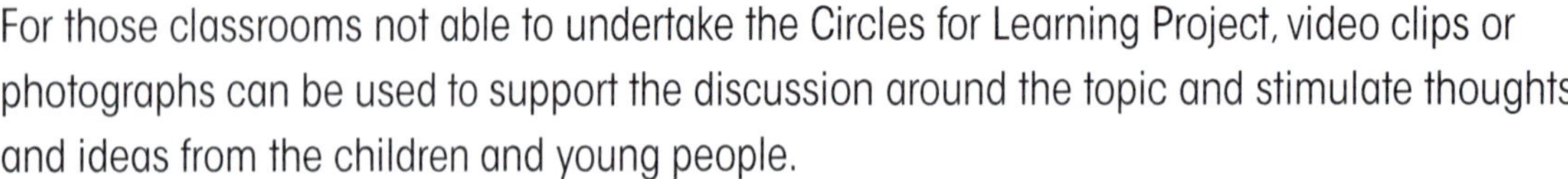

For those classrooms not able to undertake the Circles for Learning Project, video clips or photographs can be used to support the discussion around the topic and stimulate thoughts and ideas from the children and young people.

Task

KS2/3: To create a flow diagram of behaviour and explore when and which strategies would help.

1. Watch the video of a child becoming frustrated because she is not able to put the boots on, https://www.youtube.com/watch?v=2F5ScH21IK8

   or the baby with a shape sorter
   https://www.youtube.com/watch?v=lwHX15K-c5w

2. Imagine this behaviour as a flow diagram and draw this together in class.
3. Think of the different things that could have happened in different places that may have affected the baby – did they make him/her feel better or worse?
4. What might the parent have been feeling?
5. What strategies seemed to work for the baby?
6. When you get fed up, down or angry with the world, which strategies work for you?
7. Work in small groups to complete a first aid box of strategies – this can contain chocolate!!
8. Share and discuss what the young people have come up with. Talk about strategies that are positive – talking to friends and for KS3 ones that are not positive – drinking, smoking, drugs etc.
9. Good support systems are a way to stay positive and look after your wellbeing.
10. Remind the young people of our thought processes and rumination – how can they give themselves a break from this when they need to? Stop the thought – when the thought comes just say STOP in their head. If it returns say STOP again. It will soon get the message. Think of other things that you can do when you're preoccupied with non-helpful thoughts.
11. Work, focus on other things, go out with friends, do activities that you enjoy like reading a book, watching a film.

RESOURCES

1. My First Aid Kit
2. Pens, pencils
3. Video clips
4. Flow chart of child playing with toy

IMPORTANT POINTS

- It is important to develop a range of strategies and self-support systems that you can use when you need them.

LEARNING LINKS

Creativity, learning relationships, meaning making, emotional literacy.

REFLECTION

Questions:

Positive comment from child:

Positive comment from adult:

LEARNING DIMENSIONS		SOCIAL & EMOTIONAL SKILLS	
Strategic awareness		Emotional literacy	
Learning relationships		Neuroscience	
Curiosity		Self-regulation	
Creativity		Self-development	
Meaning making			
Changing & learning			
Resilience			

Baby's Feelings	Actions	Mum's Feelings
	Baby playing with shape sorter	
	Shape wouldn't go into the hole	
	Baby bashes the shape on the shape sorter	
	Baby cries and looks at Mum. Mum doesn't respond.	
	Baby tries again, still unable to put the shape in the shape sorter, but drops shape into the top of the toy.	
	Mum comments 'Oh dear'	
	Baby tries again but still is not able to get the shape in and so screeches	
	Mum says 'let me help' and puts the shape near the hole	
	Baby still is not able to and makes more noise	
	Take a break	

MY FIRST AID KIT

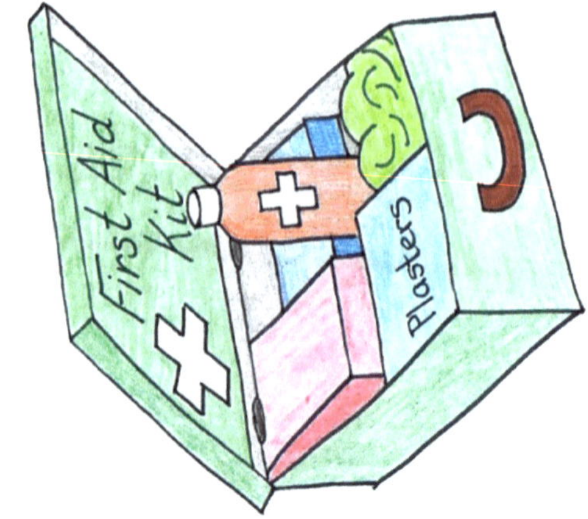
First Aid Kit
Plasters

The emotional alarm system

SESSION OBJECTIVES

To understand how we can control our emotions.

SESSION OUTCOMES

✓ Know which part of our brain is responsible for our emotions – the amygdala.

✓ Know that our brain is trying to protect us and so releases chemicals into our body to help.

✓ Know that emotions are the consequence of something and that we have control over them – if we can get thinking brain back online.

✓ Illustration of brain releasing chemicals.

LESSON PLAN

➢ Ask the children to think about a time when they saw their class baby become overwhelmed.

➢ Discuss what they observed and how baby tried to cope and then what their parent did.

For those classrooms not able to undertake the Circles for Learning Project, video clips or photographs can be used to support the discussion around the topic and stimulate thoughts and ideas from the children and young people.

Task

KS2/3: To create a cartoon to show what happens when the amygdala is triggered and believes the body is under threat.

1. Show the children a picture of the amygdala in the brain.
   http://www.wired.co.uk/news/archive/2013-02/04/amygdala-brain-fear-centre-mystery

2. Explore, through discussion, how the brain looks after us and that it wants to protect us. It keeps track of all the information coming into our body via our senses and looks for rewards or threats.

3. Display pictures of different things (crocodile, cake, bat, spider, apple, book) and ask what emotions they would cause – reward or threat.

4. Watch the brain YouTube clip about the amygdala and how it hijacks the thinking brain. The emotional brain, https://www.youtube.com/watch?v=xNYOAAUtH3g.

5. Ask the children to illustrate the brain receiving information from the senses and then releasing the chemicals as cartoon characters to get the body ready for flight or fight.

RESOURCES

1. Large flip chart
2. Pens for flip chart
3. Pictures of reward or threat
4. Amygdala
5. Brain
6. Reward or threat cartoon sheet

IMPORTANT POINTS

The **amygdala** is an almond-shaped structure in the brain; its name comes from the Greek word for 'almond'. As with most other brain structures, you actually have two amygdalae. Each amygdala is located close to the hippocampus, in the frontal portion of the temporal lobe.

Your amygdalae are essential to your ability to feel certain emotions and to perceive them in other people. This includes fear and the many changes that it causes in the body. If you are being followed at night by a suspicious-looking individual and your heart is pounding, chances are that your amygdalae are very active!

Our brain looks for rewards or threats. If it sees a threat it releases chemicals to help us manage that threat. It gets us ready to **Fight, Flight, Freeze or Flock.** The chemicals it releases are cortisol and adrenaline.

If our brain sees a reward – something that we like – it releases serotonin and dopamine. These are the pleasure chemicals.

Our emotional brain will often hijack our thinking brain. Our behaviour can sometimes get us into trouble because of this.

LEARNING LINKS

Speaking and listening, literacy, Science.

REFLECTION

Questions:

Positive comment from child:

Positive comment from adult:

LEARNING DIMENSIONS		SOCIAL & EMOTIONAL SKILLS	
Strategic awareness		Emotional literacy	
Learning relationships		Neuroscience	
Curiosity		Self-regulation	
Creativity		Self-development	
Meaning making			
Changing & learning			
Resilience			

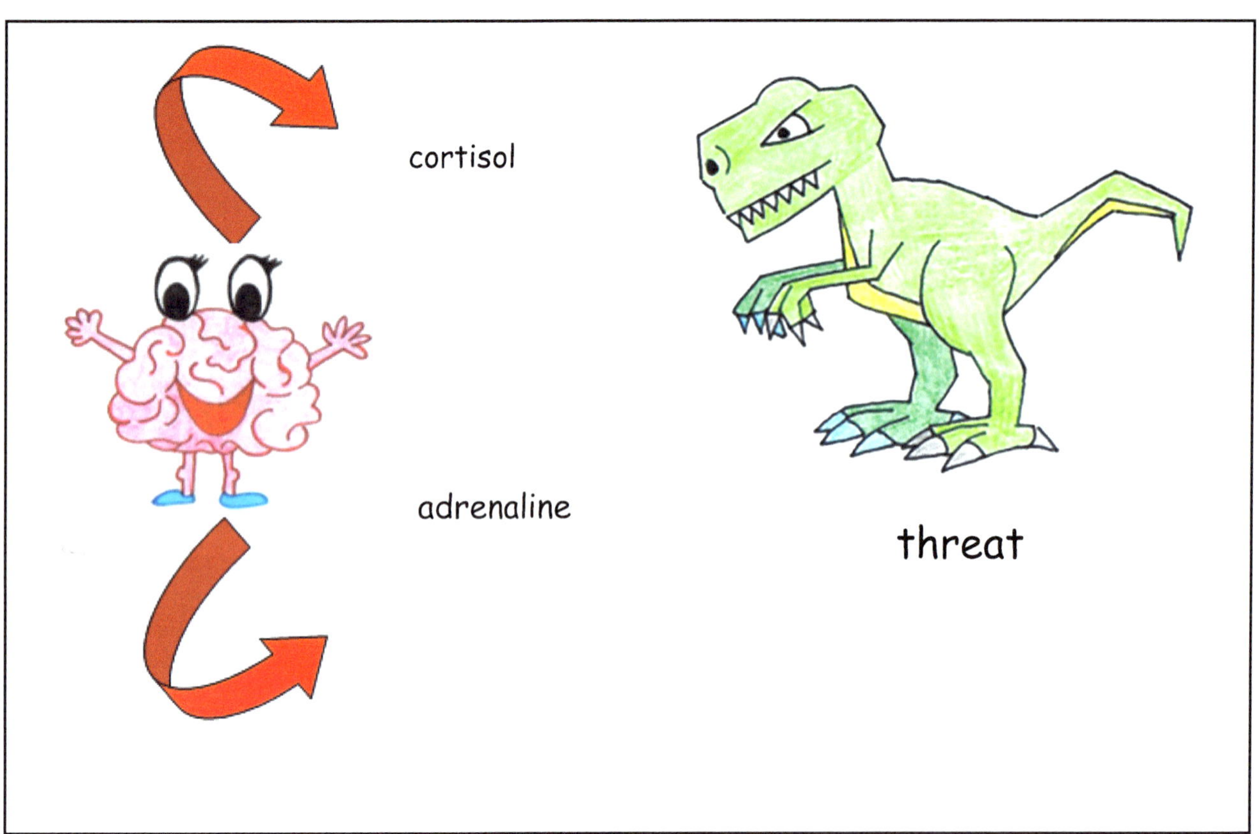
cortisol
adrenaline
threat

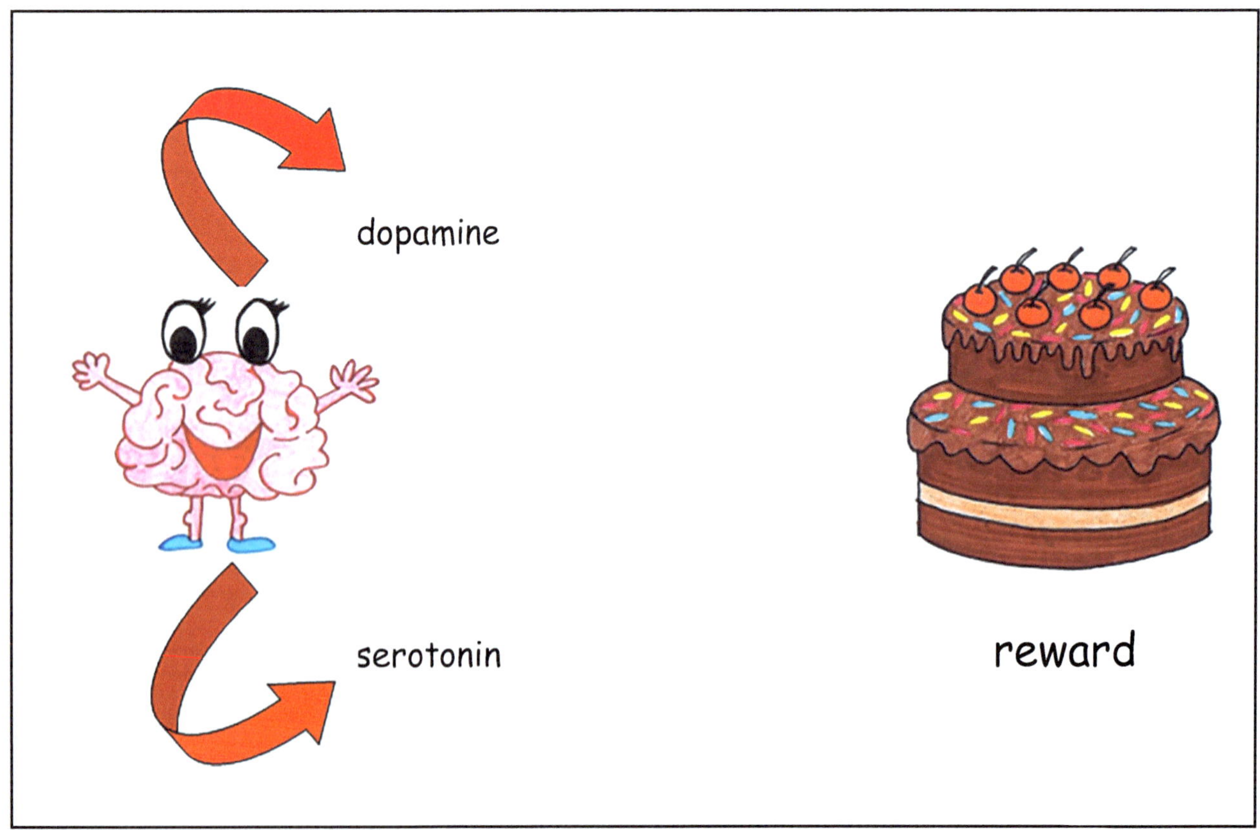
dopamine
serotonin
reward

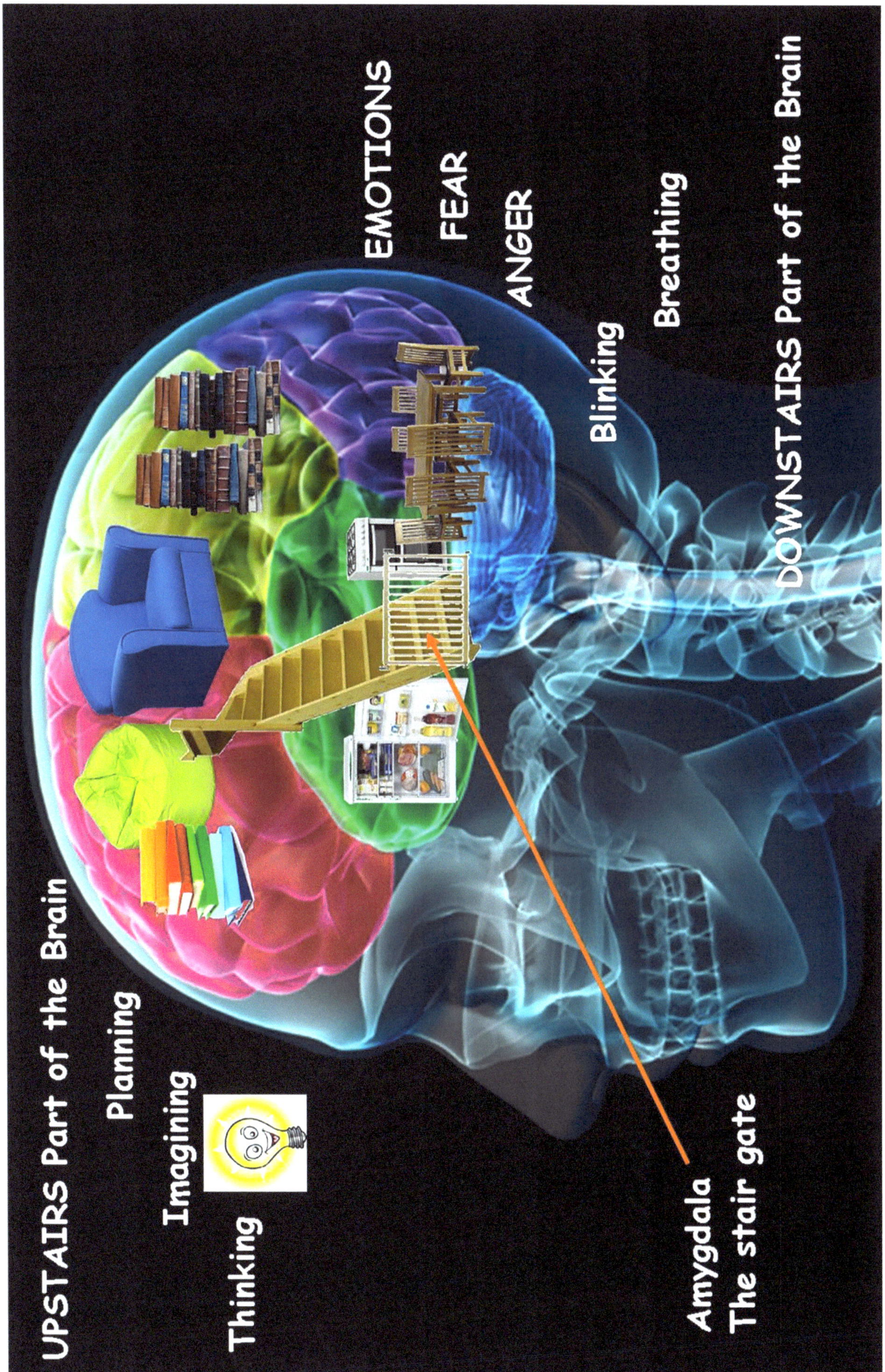

UPSTAIRS Part of the Brain

Planning

Imagining

Thinking

EMOTIONS

FEAR

ANGER

Blinking

Breathing

DOWNSTAIRS Part of the Brain

Amygdala
The stair gate

Creative meditation on the soles of my feet

SESSION OBJECTIVES

To learn that the brain and body both need regular focused down-time to be able to work and learn effectively.

SESSION OUTCOMES

- ✓ An unobtrusive meditation.
- ✓ Experience relaxation.

LESSON PLAN

- ➢ Ask the children to remember a time when their class baby was very excitable. How did the parent calm them.
- ➢ What sort of emotional state did their class baby need to be in to be able to learn?

For those classrooms not able to undertake the Circles for Learning Project, video clips or photographs can be used to support the discussion around the topic and stimulate thoughts and ideas from the children and young people.

Task

KS1: To be able to share how they feel on their Energiser and discuss ways to calm.
KS2/3: Meditation on the soles of my feet.

KS1

1. Remind the children about the different states that they can experience – calm, focused, excited, etc.
2. Discuss which state is better for learning.
3. Discuss how the children get themselves into a learning state.

4. Tell the children you have an experiment for them to try as a way of getting them into the learning zone.

5. Give each table the feet picture.

6. Share the meditation focusing on the soles of their feet. Work with the whole class and go through the meditation of the soles of the feet.

KS2

1. Show the children a range of pictures and ask them to choose the most relaxing ones.

2. Play a range of music and ask them to choose the most restful pieces.

3. Remind the children of the arousal zones.

4. Discuss visualisation and relaxation and explain why it is important for the brain to rest and recharge and to calm when too excited or experiencing a high emotion.

5. Ask the question 'How good would it be if you were in charge of your own Energiser?'

6. Get the children to draw their Energiser.

7. Ask the children to mark where they are on their Energiser at different times of the day.

8. Share different strategies that the children use to get them into their Learning Zone.

KS2/3

1. Ask the young people to plot their arousal levels throughout a lesson. Discuss how they change, with natural highs and lows and how the children and young people manage these. What do they use to 'pep' them up? What do you use? What do they use to calm? What do you use?

2. Introduce them to the meditation on the soles of their feet and ask them to test it out.

3. Read the meditation at the end of the session and ask them to have a go at different times when they need to calm – when they are upset, angry or becoming stressed. Ask the children and young people to share these examples at the next lesson. Use this meditation at the beginning of the next lesson.

RESOURCES

1. Large flip chart

2. Pens for flip chart

3. Sticky notes

4. Paper and pens
5. Coloured pens
6. Feet picture
7. Arousal zones
8. Video of the soles of the feet meditation, https://www.youtube.com/watch?v=cj3nS5y8TD4
9. Soles of the feet meditation

IMPORTANT POINTS

- Steps to relaxation.
- Working together.

LEARNING LINKS

Speaking and listening, collaboration, information processing, questioning, observation, creativity, planning and organisation.

REFLECTION

Questions:

Positive comment from child:

Positive comment from adult:

LEARNING DIMENSIONS		SOCIAL & EMOTIONAL SKILLS	
Strategic awareness		Emotional literacy	
Learning relationships		Neuroscience	
Curiosity		Self-regulation	
Creativity		Self-development	
Meaning making			
Changing & learning			
Resilience			

Arousal zones

ENERGY LEVELS

Over Active Zone Hyperactive

Optimal Learning Zone

Under Active Zone Hypoactive

TIME

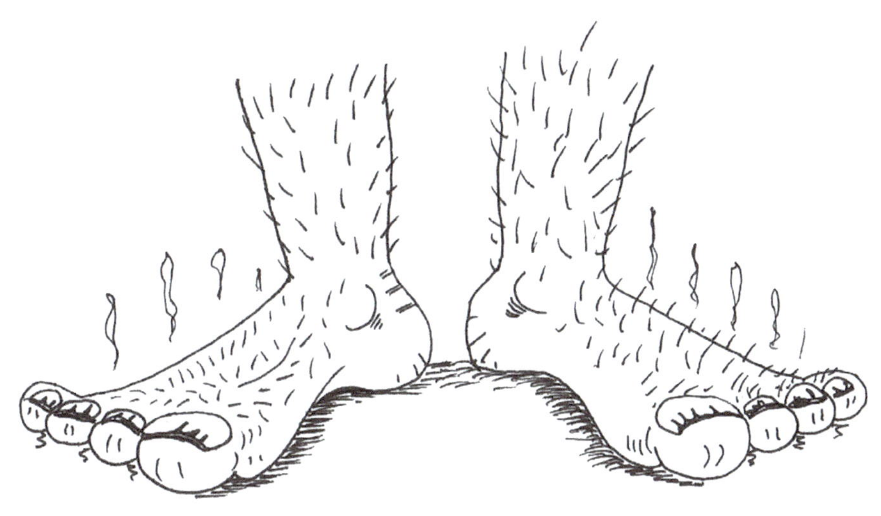

SOLES OF THE FEET MEDITATION

1. If you are standing, stand in a natural relaxed posture with your arms hanging by your sides and your knees slightly bent and with the soles of your feet flat on the floor.
2. If you are sitting, sit comfortably with the soles of your feet flat on the floor.
3. Breathe naturally, and do nothing.
4. Now, shift all your attention to the soles of your feet.
5. Slowly, move your toes.
6. Feel your shoes covering your feet, feel the texture of your socks or tights.
7. Notice the temperature of your feet – warm or cool.
8. Notice how light or heavy they feel.
9. Now notice the connection with the surface beneath your feet.
10. Take a moment and focus on how your feet feel.
11. Feel the heels of your feet against the back of your shoes. If you do not have shoes on, feel the floor or carpet with the soles of your feet.
12. Slow down your breathing a little and notice it as it enters and flows into your lungs.
13. Breathe out in a slow breath and notice how it leaves your lungs, flowing out of your nose.
14. Do this three times.
15. Now, gradually let yourself think and see the room in which you are in. Think about your whole body; when you are ready give your hands a shake and then notice how you feel in comparison to how you felt when you started.

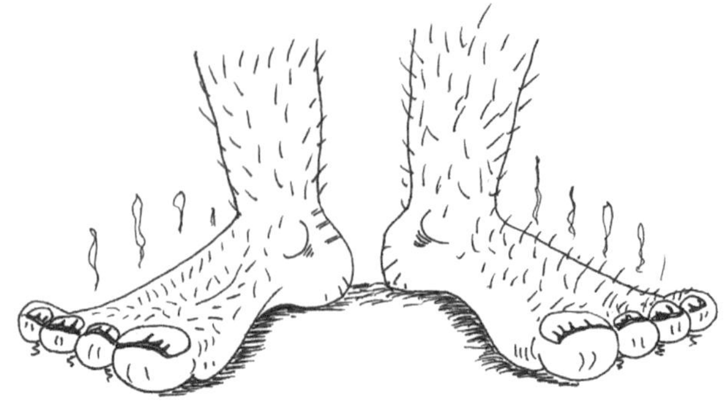

A sensory safari   

SESSION OBJECTIVES

To learn that the brain and body both need regular focused down-time to be able to work and learn effectively.

SESSION OUTCOMES

- ✓ A fun way to relax and focus on the senses.
- ✓ Experience relaxation.

LESSON PLAN

- ➢ Ask the children to remember a time when their class baby was overwhelmed or flooded with an emotion.
- ➢ What did the parent do to help them calm?

For those classrooms not able to undertake the Circles for Learning Project, video clips or photographs can be used to support the discussion around the topic and stimulate thoughts and ideas from the children and young people.

Task

KS1/KS2: To explore different states of mind and strategies that support us in changing states. KS3: To practise the ability to think about the information the body is receiving via the senses as a way to relax.

KS1/2

Working in teams, ask the children to link the words and pictures and smells. Give the children a selection of old magazines and ask them to cut out words and pictures and put them onto 3 A3 pages, one marked 'Relaxed', one marked 'Exhilarated' and one marked 'Focused'.

- Relaxed
- Exhilarated
- Focused

Share the arousal graph with the children and discuss where they do their best learning.

Ask them to share how they get from one stage to another – what strategies do they use?

Excited to Focused

Focused to Calm

Calm to Focused

Focused to Excited

1. Tell the children that you are going to take them on a sensory safari.

2. Discuss what the 7 senses are – sight, sound, smell, taste, touch, vestibular and proprioception.

3. Explain that Safi means journey in Kiswahili and that you are going to take them on a journey around school and you want them to focus on the different things that their senses notice.

4. Walk the children through school and then out into a quiet garden or field. Stand and let them listen.

5. Return to the class and then sit in a circle and share what they have experienced.

6. Ask the children to explain how they felt before, during and after the safari.

7. This can be used at any time in class by walking around or just sitting and letting the senses collect and notice things.

KS3

1. Ask the children and young people to share a time when they feel energised, calm and focused.

2. Put their ideas on different coloured sticky notes under the 3 headings.

3. Ask if the children and young people can take themselves to any of the areas when they want?

4. What do they have to do to get there?

5. Introduce the Sensory 4 by 4. Ask the children and young people to take a moment and to just become aware of the information that is being collected by their body and thought about by the brain. Ask them to find 4 things for each area.

6. Set the clock for 1 minute.

7. Share what they noticed.

8. Share how they changed their state before and after the exercise.

RESOURCES

1. Large flip chart
2. Pens for flip chart
3. Sticky notes
4. Paper and pens
5. Coloured pens
6. Computer access
7. Selection of magazines and holiday brochures.
8. Lavender, lemon, mint, coffee, vanilla, basil scents or objects.

IMPORTANT POINTS

- Steps to relaxation.
- Working together.

LEARNING LINKS

Speaking and listening, collaboration, information processing, questioning, observation, creativity, planning and organisation.

REFLECTION

Questions:

Positive comment from child:

Positive comment from adult:

LEARNING DIMENSIONS		SOCIAL & EMOTIONAL SKILLS	
Strategic awareness		Emotional literacy	
Learning relationships		Neuroscience	
Curiosity		Self-regulation	
Creativity		Self-development	
Meaning making			
Changing & learning			
Resilience			

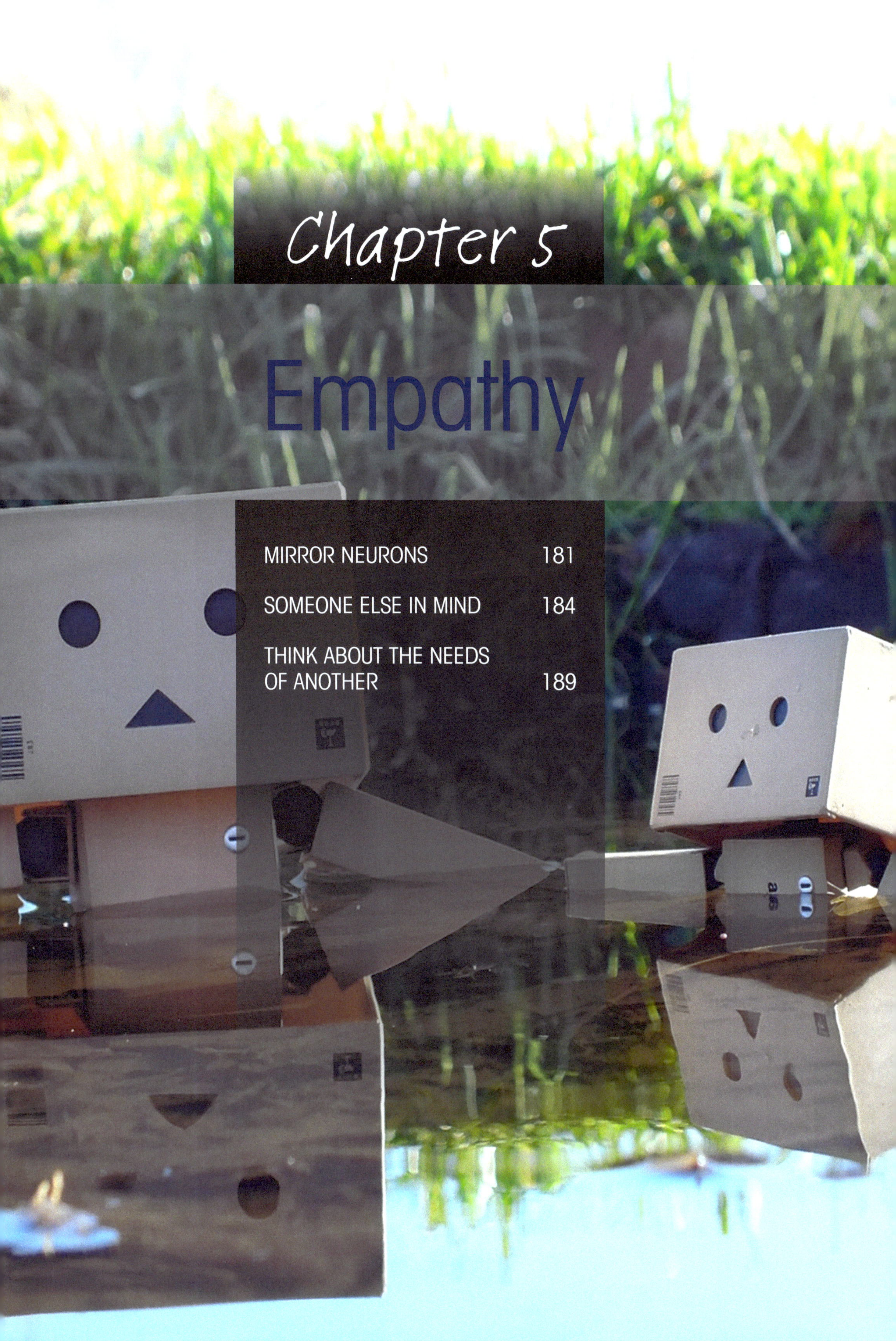

Chapter 5

Empathy

Mirror neurons

SESSION OBJECTIVES

To investigate how we learn to empathise with others, understand how they are feeling.

SESSION OUTCOMES

- ✓ To create a poster that shows what empathy is, how it develops and why developing this skill is very important.

LESSON PLAN

- ➢ Ask the children to watch the parent and baby's facial expressions – what do they notice? Help children to observe the similarities in faces – the mirroring.

For those classrooms not able to undertake the Circles for Learning Project, video clips or photographs can be used to support the discussion around the topic and stimulate thoughts and ideas from the children and young people.

Task

KS2/3: To make a poster explaining what mirror neurons are and how they impact on the way we respond to others.

1. Show the two video clips and discuss the monkey experiment.
2. Share the video clips on mirror neurons and discuss.
3. Link back to the work on body language and interactions with others.
4. Pose the question what would happen if the parent was suffering from depression or was preoccupied with health or the loss of a close family member?
5. Discuss the implications of mirror neurons to baby development.

6. Create a poster explaining what mirror neurons are – agree the criteria for this together.
7. When completed, share the work and discuss.

RESOURCES

1. Large flip chart
2. Pens for flip chart
3. Sticky notes
4. Paper and pens
5. Photos of parent and baby mirroring each other's faces
6. 'The empathic civilisation', https://www.youtube.com/watch?v=l7AWnfFRc7g
7. 'Mirror neurons part 1', https://www.youtube.com/watch?v=XzMqPYfeA-s
8. 'Mirror neurons part 2', https://www.youtube.com/watch?v=xmEsGQ3JmKg

IMPORTANT POINTS

- To understand how mirror neurons support us understanding another person and the benefits for this.
- Linking our emotional response and behaviour to others.

LEARNING LINKS

Speaking and listening, collaboration, information processing, questioning, observation, creativity, planning and organisation, teamwork.

REFLECTION

Questions:

Positive comment from child:

Positive comment from adult:

LEARNING DIMENSIONS		SOCIAL & EMOTIONAL SKILLS	
Strategic awareness		Emotional literacy	
Learning relationships		Neuroscience	
Curiosity		Self-regulation	
Creativity		Self-development	
Meaning making			
Changing & Learning			
Resilience			

Someone else in mind

SESSION OBJECTIVES

To think about the wants and needs of others allows us to develop and strengthen our ability to empathise and understand others.

SESSION OUTCOMES

✓ To create a gift for a friend or person who is known.

LESSON PLAN

➢ Ask the children and young people what they notice about the interactions between their class baby and its parents.

➢ Support them observing the intimate looks and gestures.

➢ How do the parents know what the baby needs when the baby cannot talk?

➢ Support a discussion about empathy.

For those classrooms not able to undertake the Circles for Learning Project, video clips or photographs can be used to support the discussion around the topic and stimulate thoughts and ideas from the children and young people.

Task

KS2/3: To create an imaginary gift for someone that they know.

1. Recap on what empathy is and how we are able to 'feel' what another person is feeling by watching them and experiencing their feelings with our mirror neurons.

2. Discuss what you might give a friend/family member that would reflect what they like or need, T-Shirt, cap, cup, pencil case for example and how you could design it just for them. Dad might like barbecues and so you might put hot-dogs on his T-Shirt.

RESOURCES

1. Paper, pens
2. T-Shirt template, hat template, cup template and pencil case template
3. Sticky notes
4. Coloured pencils

IMPORTANT POINTS

- To understand how listening and paying attention to what people tell us as well as watching and noticing body language and facial expressions can help us understand and know someone.
- Linking our emotional response to others and our behaviour.

LEARNING LINKS

Speaking and listening, collaboration, information processing, questioning, observation, creativity, planning and organisation, teamwork.

REFLECTION

Questions:

Positive comment from child:

Positive comment from adult:

LEARNING DIMENSIONS		SOCIAL & EMOTIONAL SKILLS	
Strategic awareness		Emotional literacy	
Learning relationships		Neuroscience	
Curiosity		Self-regulation	
Creativity		Self-development	
Meaning making			
Changing & learning			
Resilience			

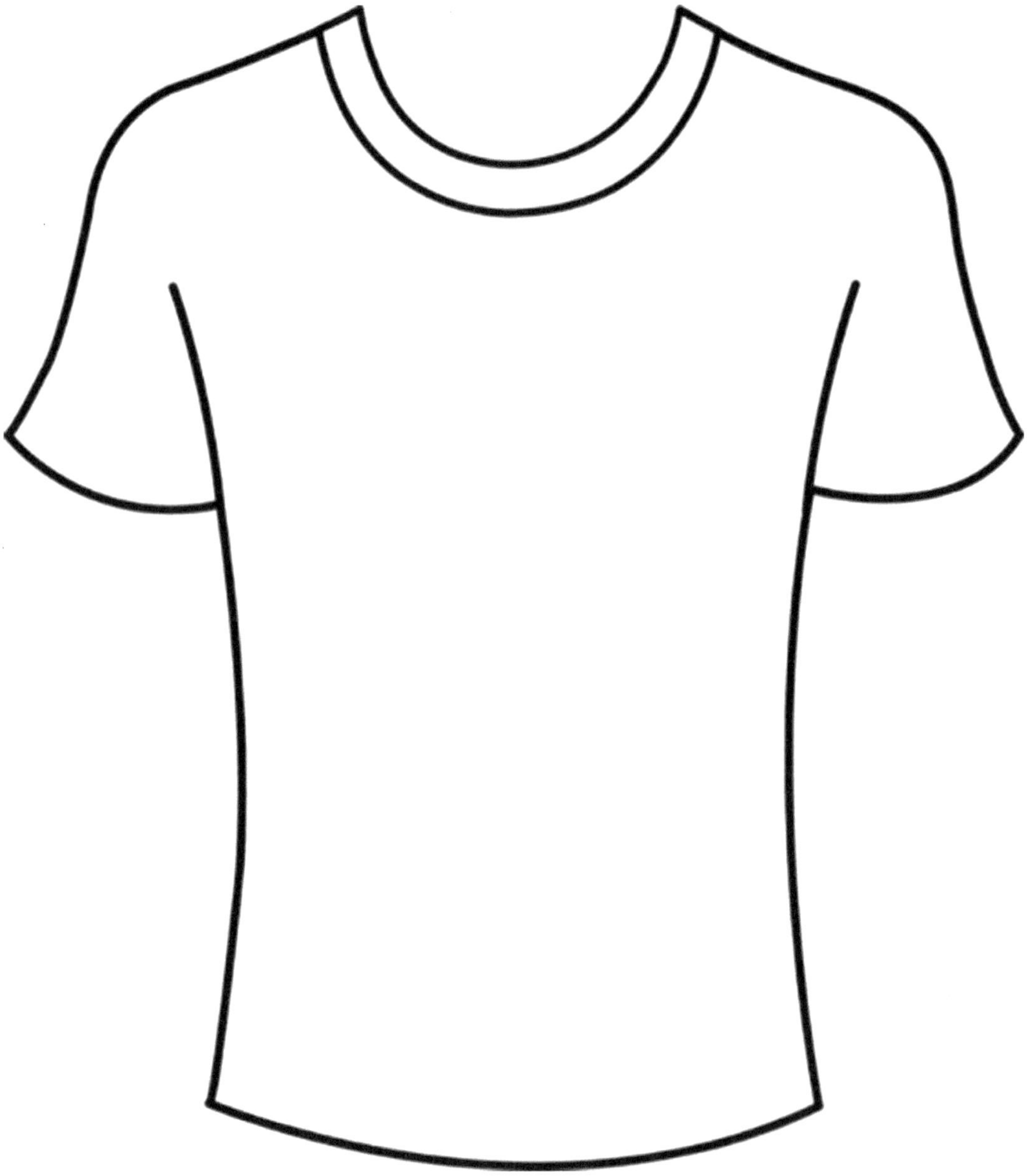

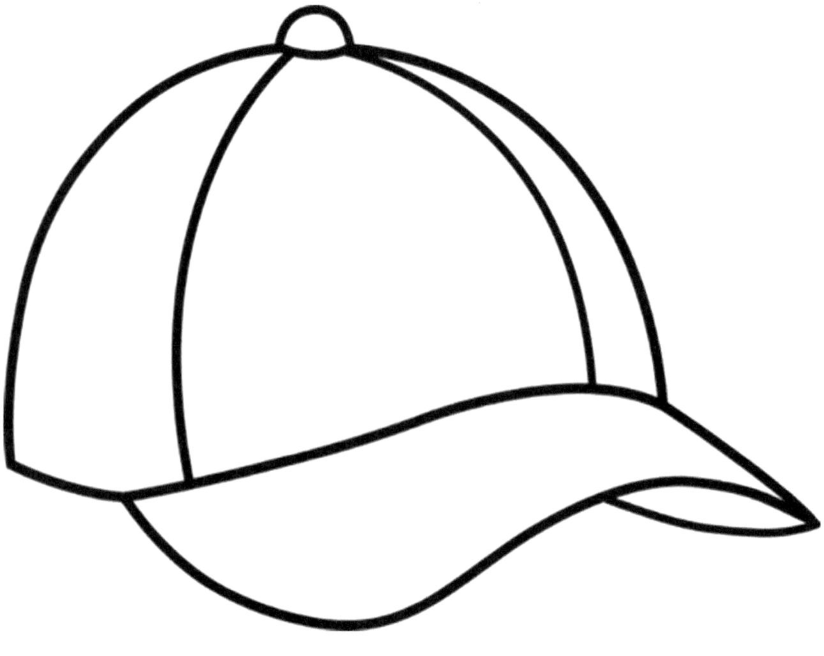

Think about the needs of another

SESSION OBJECTIVES

To think about another person and identify what they might like or need.

SESSION OUTCOMES

✓ To think about someone they know and give them 3 magic stars.

✓ To create 3 lucky stars for a character or person.

✓ To be able to describe why they had chosen the lucky stars they had for their character or person.

LESSON PLAN

➢ Remind the children of a time when their class baby's parent was trying to work out what the baby wanted – discuss how she/he could do this.

➢ Help the children think about how our experiences help us to understand others and about out mirror neurons that help us understand how someone else may be feeling.

For those classrooms not able to undertake the Circles for Learning Project, video clips or photographs can be used to support the discussion around the topic and stimulate thoughts and ideas from the children and young people.

Task

KS1/KS2/KS3: To be able to think about someone they know and imagine what they might like or need.

KS1/KS2

1. Share a variety of pictures with the children of different people and discuss what they might be feeling and what they could do to help, e.g. a street cleaner in the rain might like a flask of tea.

2. For the younger children, ask them to think about someone from their family and identify 3 magic stars or gifts they would give them e.g. Mum – a new washing machine, a day at the seaside and a chef for the day to make her dinner!

3. For the older children – put them in groups of 4–6 and ask them to choose a card from the character pack, and then create 3 magic stars that they would like or might need e.g. a dog – a bone, a walk or to sleep on the children's bed.

4. When the children have finished their stars ask them to share who they chose and then what wishes they gave them.

5. At the end of the session ask the children to share What Went Well (WWW) for them.

KS3

1. Ask the young people to think of a friend and, if money was no object, what would they give them – 3 stars. This could be real or imaginary or magical. If they had a friend who loved dancing they might let them be a contestant on *Dancing on Ice*.

RESOURCES

1. Large flip chart

2. Pens for flip chart

3. Sticky notes

4. Paper and pens

5. Stars

6. A collection of photos that show conflict or scenes where people would have different views or opinions

7. A selection of different characters – dog, cat, superhero, the tooth fairy, one of the 3 little pigs, Cinderella, Harry Potter, the Easter Bunny, a turkey at Christmas

IMPORTANT POINTS

- To explore how another person might feel.

- By thinking about other people we might want to change our behaviour.

LEARNING LINKS

Speaking and listening, collaboration, information processing, questioning, observation, creativity, planning and organisation, teamwork.

REFLECTION

Questions:

Positive comment from child:

Positive comment from adult:

LEARNING DIMENSIONS		SOCIAL & EMOTIONAL SKILLS	
Strategic awareness		Emotional literacy	
Learning relationships		Neuroscience	
Curiosity		Self-regulation	
Creativity		Self-development	
Meaning making			
Changing & learning			
Resilience			

My person

Bibliography

Al-Ghani, K. I. (2008). *The Red Beast: Controlling Anger in Children with Asperger's Syndrome.* London: Jessica Kingsley Publishers.

'Baby frustrated with toy', https://www.youtube.com/watch?v=lwHX15K-c5w (accessed 24 September 2018).

'Baby gets frustrated', https://www.youtube.com/watch?v=2F5ScH21lK8 (accessed 24 September 2018).

Cassity, J. (n.d.). 'How to cultivate an attitude of gratitude', https://my.happify.com/hd/cultivate-an-attitude-of-gratitude/ (accessed 24 September 2018).

Emmons, R. (2010). 'Why gratitude is good', *Greater Good Magazine*, https://greatergood.berkeley.edu/article/item/why_gratitude_is_good/ (accessed 24 September 2018).

Gardner, H. and Hatch, T. (1989). 'Multiple intelligences go to school: Educational implications for the theory of multiple intelligences', *Educational Researcher* 18 (8), November.

Goleman, D. (2004). *Emotional Intelligence and Working with Emotional Intelligence.* London: Bloomsbury Publishing.

Kelly, M. (2009). *Why Am I Here?* Cincinnati: Beacon Childrens.

Lee, S. (2008). *Wave.* San Francisco: Chronicle Books.

Mayer, J. D. and Cobb, C. D. (2000). 'Educational policy on emotional intelligence: Does it make sense?', *Educational Psychology Review* 12 (2), pp. 163–183.

'Mindful moment Monday: Soles of the feet', November 2013, https://www.youtube.com/watch?v=cj3nS5y8TD4 (accessed 24 September 2018).

'Mirror neurons part 1', https://www.youtube.com/watch?v=XzMqPYfeA-s (accessed 24 September 2018).

'Mirror neurons part 2', https://www.youtube.com/watch?v=xmEsGQ3JmKg (accessed 24 September 2018).

Rosen, M. and Blake, Q. (2011). *Michael Rosen's Sad Book.* London: Walker Books.

Science Alert, 'Watch: What is a thought made of?', https://www.sciencealert.com/watch-what-is-a-thought-made-of (accessed 24 September 2018).

SEAL: Photocards of Feelings: Primary. https://www.tes.com/teaching-resource/seal-photocards-of-feelings-primary-6095733 (accessed 24 September 2018).

Smallwood, B. and Kilborn, S. 'Success' rainbow poem. http://www.dyslexia.tv/freethinkersu/wisdom_success_smallwood.htm (accessed 24 September 2018).

Steadman, I. (2013). 'Study: People without brain's "fear centre" can still be scared', *Wired,* February 13, http://www.wired.co.uk/news/archive/2013-02/04/amygdala-brain-fear-centre-mystery (accessed 24 September 2018).

'The emotional brain', https://www.youtube.com/watch?v=xNYOAAUtH3g (accessed 24 September 2018).

'The empathic civilisation', Jeremy Rifkin, https://www.youtube.com/watch?v=l7AWnfFRc7g (accessed 24 September 2018).

'The exam. Mr Bean Official', https://www.youtube.com/watch?v=9LhLjpsstPY (accessed 24 September 2018).

Weare, K. (2004). *Developing the Emotionally Literate School.* London: Sage Publications.

Williamson, M. (1992). 'Our deepest fear' in Marianne Williamson, *A Return to Love: Reflections on the Principles of 'A Course in Miracles'.* New York: HarperCollins, pp. 190–191.

mater o **FFAITH**

Pobl

LL

Llawlyfr ar gy

Non ap Emlyn

Cyhoeddwyd gan Gyd-bwyllgor Addysg Cymru (WJEC CBAC Cyf.)
245 Rhodfa'r Gorllewin
Caerdydd CF5 2YX

Mae Uned Iaith Genedlaethol Cymru yn rhan o WJEC CBAC Limited, elusen gofrestredig a chwmni a gyfyngir gan warant ac a reolir gan awdurdodau lleol Cymru.

Comisiynwyd gyda chymorth ariannol Awdurdod Cymwysterau, Cwricwlwm ac Asesu Cymru.

Dyluniwyd gan Mostyn Davies, CBAC

Lluniau'r clawr: Empics UCh; *The Star,* Kuala Lumpur, Malaysia UD;
Camera Press/Dan Chung/GM GCh; Empics GD.

Argraffwyd gan Wasg Gomer, Llandysul, Ceredigion, SA44 4JL

ISBN 1 86085 609 8

Cynnwys

Rhagymadrodd

Prif nod cyfres *Mater o Ffaith* yw denu disgyblion ail iaith Cyfnodau Allweddol 3 a 4 i ddarllen deunyddiau ffeithiol yn y Gymraeg. Mae'n cynnwys llyfrau sy'n ymwneud â thair thema:

- Adeiladau
- Pobl
- Hamddena.

Yn ogystal, ceir **Llawlyfr ar gyfer athrawon** ar gyfer pob thema.

Er mwyn apelio at ystod y disgyblion yng Nghyfnodau Allweddol 3 a 4, mae iaith y llyfrau wedi ei strwythuro'n ofalus fel bod pedwar llyfr ar bob thema, gyda phob llyfr wedi ei ysgrifennu ar gyfer lefel wahanol, sef:

- Lefelau 3/4
- Lefelau 4/5
- Lefelau 5/6
- Lefelau 6/7

Mae'n bosibl darllen y darnau fel dosbarth cyfan, drwy rannu'r dosbarth yn grwpiau, neu drwy roi llyfrau i unigolion eu darllen. Yn wir, mae testun y llyfrau wedi ei drefnu mewn blociau o wybodaeth yn aml iawn, fel bod modd darllen cymaint neu cyn lleied ag sy'n briodol, e.e. gall rhai disgyblion ddarllen unedau cyfan tra gall grwpiau neu unigolion eraill ddarllen darn(au) penodol.

Yn y **Llawlyfr ar gyfer athrawon**, ceir syniadau ynglŷn â chysylltu'r darnau ffeithiol â gwaith arall a wneir yn yr ystafell ddosbarth, ynghyd â syniadau am weithgareddau pellach sy'n cyd-fynd â'r wybodaeth sy'n cael ei chyflwyno. Fodd bynnag, pwysleisir mai syniadau'n unig a geir yma a bod croeso i athrawon ddefnyddio'r gwaith yn y modd sydd fwyaf priodol i'w sefyllfa nhw, gan ddewis o blith y gweithgareddau a'u haddasu, yn unol â gofynion eu dosbarthiadau.

Gobeithir, hefyd, y bydd disgyblion eu hunain yn troi at y llyfrau hyn ac yn eu darllen o ran diddordeb gan fod ynddynt wybodaeth ddiddorol a pherthnasol.

Pobl Llyfrau1-4: agweddau cyffredin

Er bod cynnwys y llyfrau'n amrywio'n fawr, mae cysylltiad rhwng rhai unedau fel bod dosbarth cyfan yn medru darllen am agwedd gyffredin ar y thema ***Pobl*** *yr un pryd. Gall hyn arwain at waith grŵp diddorol wrth i grwpiau gwahanol gael cyfle i gyfnewid gwybodaeth am yr hyn maen nhw wedi ei ddarllen.*

AGWEDDAU CYFFREDIN I BOB LEFEL

- **Pobl â doniau arbennig**

Lefelau 3/4: Waw – Pobl fagnetig!

Lefelau 4/5: Waw – gweld tu mewn i bobl!

Lefelau 5/6: Rhyfedd!

Lefelau 6/7: Sarah Jacob

- **Dyfeiswyr**

Lefelau 3/4: László Bíró, Marcel Bich, Bette Nesmith Graham

Lefelau 4/5: Jules Léotard, William Russell Frisbie

Lefelau 5/6: Levi Strauss

Lefelau 6/7: Candido Jacuzzi

- **Pobl sy wedi sefydlu cwmnïau llwyddiannus**

Lefelau 3/4: Doug Perkins (Specsavers)

Lefelau 4/5: Teulu Kellogg

Pobl

Lefelau 5/6: Teulu Cadbury

Lefelau 6/7: Clarence Birdseye

- **Enwogion o Gymru / Pobl enwog â chysylltiad â Chymru**

Lefelau 3/4: Catrin Finch, Colin Jackson a Suzanne Packer

Lefelau 4/5: Catherine Zeta-Jones

Lefelau 5/6: J.K. Rowling

Lefelau 6/7: Helen Willetts, Derek Brockway a Siân Lloyd

- **Pobl sy'n helpu pobl eraill**

Lefelau 4/5: Nicole Cooke

Lefelau 5/6: Bob Geldof KBE

Lefelau 6/7: Syr Ranulph Fiennes

Pobl Llyfr 1

Lefelau 3/4

Ceir chwech o unedau am wahanol bobl, sef:

- Waw – Pobl fagnetig!
- Colin Jackson
- Suzanne Packer
- Catrin Finch
- Y Cas Pensiliau
  - László Bíró
  - Marcel Bich
  - Bette Nesmith Graham
- Doug Perkins

Waw - Pobl fagnetig! (tt. 3-4)

Gallech chi ddechrau drwy:

- ddod â chasgliad o bethau metel i'r wers, mewn bocs, a gofyn i'r dosbarth ddyfalu beth sy yno; os nad oes neb yn llwyddo, gellid rhoi cliwiau nes bod y disgyblion yn dyfalu'n gywir; yna, gellid defnyddio magnet er mwyn dangos effaith y magnet ar y metelau a chyflwyno geirfa briodol

  Neu

  dod â thudalennau o gatalog yn dangos amrywiaeth o bethau'r tŷ a gofyn i'r disgyblion restru 10 o bethau metel o'r catalog

- rhestru geiriau am bethau magnetig, e.e. nodwydd, cyllell a fforc ac ati; gellid gwneud hyn fel cystadleuaeth grwpiau, gyda'r grŵp sy'n casglu'r nifer mwyaf o eiriau'n ennill

- sôn yn gyffredinol am bobl sy'n gallu gwneud pethau anarferol, e.e. Uri Geller, Houdini, pobl sy'n rhagweld y dyfodol ac ati.

Gweithgareddau posibl sy'n deillio o'r wybodaeth

- Cyflwyno pobl sy'n / oedd yn gallu gwneud pethau anarferol eraill.

- Chwilio am fwy o wybodaeth am y rhain, ysgrifennu darnau byr amdanyn nhw a gwneud arddangosfa 'WAW!'

Pobl

Colin Jackson (t. 5)

Gallech chi ddechrau drwy:

- drafod pa chwaraeon mae'r disgyblion yn eu hoffi, faint maen nhw'n ymarfer ac ati
- rhestru pobl amlwg ym myd chwaraeon gan ddangos ym mha chwaraeon maen nhw'n cymryd rhan
- gwylio rhan o raglen deledu sy'n dangos Colin Jackson.

Gweithgareddau posibl sy'n deillio o'r wybodaeth

- Chwilio am fwy o wybodaeth am Colin Jackson ac ysgrifennu amdano.
- Chwilio am fwy o wybodaeth am Gemau Olympaidd 2012.

Suzanne Packer (t.6)

Gallech chi ddechrau drwy:

- wylio rhan o raglen deledu sy'n dangos Suzanne Packer.

Gweithgareddau posibl sy'n deillio o'r wybodaeth

- Chwilio am fwy o wybodaeth am Suzanne Packer ac ysgrifennu amdani.
- Ysgrifennu darn am raglen sy'n cynnwys Suzanne Packer.
- Edrych ar raglenni sy'n dangos pobl yn ceisio dysgu Cymraeg, eu trafod a rhoi cyngor i'r dysgwyr.

Catrin Finch (tt. 7-10)

Gallech chi ddechrau drwy:

- drafod pa fath o gerddoriaeth mae'r disgyblion yn ei hoffi, pam maen nhw'n hoffi'r gerddoriaeth yma
- gwrando ar rannau amrywiol o gryno ddisgiau Catrin Finch, mynegi barn a rhoi rheswm.

Gweithgareddau posibl sy'n deillio o'r wybodaeth

- Gwneud ymchwil bellach i fywyd a gwaith Catrin Finch.
- Paratoi proffil/erthygl amdani ar gyfer cylchgrawn.
- Gwneud 'rhaglen deledu' am Catrin Finch gyda grwpiau'n gyfrifol am wahanol agweddau ar ei gwaith.
- Ymchwilio i fywyd a gwaith cerddorion eraill o Gymru, e.e. Bryn Terfel, Cerys Matthews, Katherine Jenkins ac ati.
- Chwilio am wybodaeth ar y rhyngrwyd am gyngherddau cerddorol, hysbysebu'r cyngherddau hynny, e.e. gwneud posteri, hysbysebion, cyfweliadau radio, erthyglau ac ati.

Y Cas Pensiliau (tt. 11-16)

Gallech chi ddechrau drwy:

- ofyn i'r disgyblion restru cynnwys eu casys pensiliau.

Gweithgareddau posibl sy'n deillio o'r wybodaeth

- Chwilio am bethau eraill sydd wedi eu henwi ar ôl pobl arbennig. Gellir gwneud hyn drwy deipio *eponym* i beiriant chwilio ar y rhyngrwyd.

- Trafod y pethau hyn a gwneud arddangosfa gyda gwahanol grwpiau'n gweithio ar wahanol bethau/pobl.
- Chwilio am hanes pethau eraill mewn cas pensiliau, e.e. rwber, *post-its* ac ati.

Doug Perkins (tt.17-20)

Gallech chi ddechrau drwy:

- edrych ar luniau amrywiol o sbectols a'u disgrifio; dangos sut mae sbectols yn gallu dilyn y ffasiwn.

Gweithgareddau posibl sy'n deillio o'r wybodaeth

- Cymharu bywyd Doug Perkins yn yr ysgol â bywyd y disgyblion, e.e. faint ohonyn nhw sy'n hoffi'r un pethau â fe?
- Sôn am Tom Jones, gwrando arno'n canu a mynegi barn.
- Llunio cyfweliad gyda Doug Perkins.
- Gwneud hysbyseb am sbectols.
- Dyfeisio sbectols 'arbennig' iawn, e.e. rhai sy'n cyflawni camp arbennig (tebyg i offer 'arbennig' James Bond).
- Ymchwilio i ioga, pam mae'r gweithwyr yn gwneud ioga bob wythnos.
- Chwilio am Gymry eraill sy wedi dechrau cwmnïau, e.e. cwmnïau lleol, cenedlaethol neu ryngwladol.

Pobl Llyfr 2

Lefelau 4/5

Ceir saith o unedau am wahanol bobl, sef:

- Waw – gweld tu mewn i bobl!
- Catherine Zeta-Jones
- Nicole Cooke
- Y Leotard: Jules Léotard
- Pethau pob dydd
- Y Ffrisbi
- Beth sy i frecwast?: Teulu Kellogg

Waw - gweld tu mewn i bobl! (tt. 3-4)

Gallech chi ddechrau drwy:

- sôn yn gyffredinol am bobl sy'n gallu gwneud pethau anarferol, e.e. Uri Geller, Houdini, pobl sy'n rhagweld y dyfodol ac ati.

Gweithgareddau posibl sy'n deillio o'r wybodaeth

- Cyflwyno pobl sy'n/oedd yn gallu gwneud pethau anarferol eraill.

- Ysgrifennu darnau byr am y rhain a gwneud arddangosfa 'WAW!'

Catherine Zeta-Jones (tt. 5-8)

Gallech chi ddechrau drwy:

- drafod pa fath o ffilmiau mae'r disgyblion yn eu hoffi, pam maen nhw'n eu hoffi
- rhestru ffilmiau sy'n cynnwys Catherine Zeta-Jones
- nodi pa fath o ffilmiau ydyn nhw
- gwylio darnau o ffilmiau ar fideo a'u trafod.

Gweithgareddau posibl sy'n deillio o'r wybodaeth

- Gwneud ymchwil bellach i fywyd a gwaith Catherine Zeta-Jones.
- Paratoi proffil/erthygl amdani ar gyfer cylchgrawn.
- Gwneud 'rhaglen deledu' am Catherine Zeta-Jones gyda grwpiau'n gyfrifol am wahanol agweddau ar ei gwaith.
- Chwilio am wybodaeth am actorion eraill o Gymru, e.e. Ioan Gruffudd, Anthony Hopkins ac ati. Ceir erthyglau yn aml mewn cylchgronau fel *Iaw!* a *Lingo Newydd* ac ar wefan BBC Cymru'r Byd.

Nicole Cooke (tt.9-10)

Gallech chi ddechrau drwy:

- drafod pa chwaraeon mae'r disgyblion yn eu hoffi, faint maen nhw'n ymarfer ac ati
- rhestru pobl amlwg ym myd chwaraeon gan ddangos ym mha chwaraeon maen nhw'n cymryd rhan
- siarad yn gyffredinol am feicio, e.e. oes gan y disgyblion feic? Pa fath? Pa liw? Ble maen nhw'n beicio? Pryd? ac ati

Gweithgareddau posibl sy'n deillio o'r wybodaeth

- Gwylio cystadleuaeth feicio ar fideo a thrafod y darn.
- Ysgrifennu am daith feicio.
- Chwilio am fwy o wybodaeth am y cynllun **100% ME.**
- Gwneud posteri i gyfleu neges y cynllun **100% ME**.

Y Leotard (t.11) Jules Léotard

Gallech chi ddechrau drwy:

- drafod gwahanol fathau o ddillad chwaraeon, e.e. ydy'r disgyblion yn gwisgo dillad chwaraeon? Pryd? Ble? Pam? Oes ganddyn nhw ddillad chwaraeon sy'n cefnogi timau? Pa fath? Pa dîm? Disgrifio dillad timau pêl-droed arbennig ac ati
- trafod cost y dillad hyn
- trafod hysbysebu ar ddillad chwaraeon.

Gweithgareddau posibl sy'n deillio o'r wybodaeth

- Gwneud hysbyseb 'hen ffasiwn' am leotard yng nghyfnod Jules Léotard a hysbyseb fodern am leotard cyfoes.
- Dod o hyd i luniau o ddillad sy'n addas ar gyfer chwaraeon penodol, eu disgrifio, dweud pam maen nhw'n addas (e.e. mae leotard yn ffitio'n dynn, felly mae balerina, trapisiwr ac ati'n gallu symud yn hawdd; mae rhedwyr yn gwisgo dillad tynn er mwyn medru rhedeg yn gyflym; mae beicwyr yn gwisgo helmedau arbennig er mwyn gofalu am eu pen a theithio'n gyflym).
- Gwneud sioe dillad chwaraeon a disgrifio'r dillad.
- Hysbysebu dillad chwaraeon.
- Cynllunio dillad chwaraeon newydd.
- Chwilio am bethau eraill sydd wedi eu henwi ar ôl pobl arbennig. Gellir gwneud hyn drwy deipio *eponym* i beiriant chwilio ar y rhyngrwyd.

Y Ffrisbi (tt. 14-16)

Gallech chi ddechrau drwy:

- ofyn:
  - Ydych chi'n hoffi prynu pethau o'r siop fara / siop gacennau? Beth? Pryd? Faint mae'n gostio? Pam?
  - Ydych chi'n chwarae gyda ffrisbi weithiau? Ble? Pryd? Gyda pwy?

- Yna gellid gofyn cwestiwn pellach:
  - Beth ydy'r cysylltiad rhwng y ffrisbi a siop fara / siop gacennau, tybed?

  Gellid gofyn i grwpiau geisio gweld y cysylltiad, gwrando ar wahanol awgrymiadau ac yna troi at y darn ffeithiol.

Gweithgareddau posibl sy'n deillio o'r wybodaeth

- Gwneud hysbyseb i hysbysebu peis y *Frisbie Pie Company* / y *Pluto Platter* / y ffrisbi.

- Mae sôn yn y darn am y ffaith fod taflu ffrisbis yn gallu bod yn beryglus – gellid gwneud rheolau ynglŷn â sut i chwarae'n ddiogel, beth i wisgo ac ati.

- Chwilio am wybodaeth am gemau eraill, e.e. sut dechreuodd rygbi, gemau fel *Monopoly* ac ati a chymharu gwybodaeth.

- Chwilio am bethau eraill sydd wedi eu henwi ar ôl pobl arbennig. Gellir gwneud hyn drwy deipio *eponym* i beiriant chwilio ar y rhyngrwyd.

Beth sy i frecwast? (tt. 17-20)

Gallech chi ddechrau drwy:

- drafod beth mae'r disgyblion yn ei gael i frecwast, categoreiddio brecwast – grawnfwyd / brecwast poeth / brecwast cyflym ac ati

- dangos pam mae brecwast yn bwysig

- gwneud rhestr o'r gwahanol fathau o rawnfwydydd sy ar gael.

Gweithgareddau posibl sy'n deillio o'r wybodaeth

- Trafod grawnfwydydd – pa mor iach ydyn nhw – cymharu gwahanol rai.
- Rhoi cyngor ar sut i fwyta brecwast da, e.e. rhestr, erthygl, cyfweliad radio, taflen, hysbyseb ac ati.
- Trefnu brecwast iach / 'Cymreig' yn yr ysgol.
- Gwneud ymchwil bellach ar fywyd a gwaith teulu Kellogg.
- Ymchwilio i gwmnïau eraill sy'n gwerthu bwyd brecwast.
- Trafod dulliau *Kellogg's* o hysbysebu, edrych ar hysbysebion am wahanol fathau o fwyd brecwast sy ar y teledu a'u trafod.
- Creu hysbysebion am fwyd brecwast.
- Gwneud ymchwil i weld pa gwmnïau eraill sy wedi eu henwi ar ôl person neu deulu arbennig.

Pobl Llyfr 3 — Lefelau 5/6

Ceir pump o unedau am wahanol bobl, sef:

- Rhyfedd!
- Jîns … glas … cryf: Levi Strauss
- Siocled … siocled … a mwy o siocled!: Teulu Cadbury
- Bob Geldof KBE
- J.K. Rowling ... a ... Harry Potter

Rhyfedd! (tt. 3-6)

Gallech chi ddechrau drwy:

- chwarae cerddoriaeth o'r ffilm *Titanic*, a gofyn: O ble mae'r darn yn dod? Beth sy'n digwydd pan mae'r gerddoriaeth yn chwarae yn y ffilm?
- gwylio rhan o'r ffilm *Titanic* a'i thrafod
- casglu a chymharu gwybodaeth am y digwyddiad a'i drafod
- ysgrifennu a recordio bwletin newyddion byr am y digwyddiad
- dangos lluniau, trafod y llong, cynllunio poster i hysbysebu'r llong.

Gweithgareddau posibl sy'n deillio o'r wybodaeth

- Gwylio'r darn yn y ffilm sy'n dangos y band yn chwarae. Yna, gallai'r disgyblion feddwl am ddau gwestiwn ar gyfer cwis, e.e.

  Faint o bobl oedd yn y band?
  Faint o ddynion a faint o ferched?
  Beth oedden nhw'n wisgo?
  Beth oedden nhw'n chwarae? ac ati.

- Gwylio'r ffilm a sylwi ar rôl Arthur yn y ffilm, sef y rôl y mae Ioan Gruffudd yn ei chwarae.

- Ymchwilio mwy i hanes y *Titanic*, ysgrifennu erthygl, cyfweliad, y cofnod olaf yn nyddiadur un o'r teithwyr ac ati.

Jîns ... glas ... cryf: Levi Strauss (tt. 7-8)

Gallech chi ddechrau drwy:

- ofyn i'r disgyblion restru beth sy yn eu cwpwrdd dillad, yna, gofyn cwestiynau pellach, e.e. Pryd maen nhw'n gwisgo'r dillad yma? Beth ydy eu hoff ddillad? ac ati

- gofyn yn benodol am jîns: Pa fath sy ganddyn nhw? Faint maen nhw'n gostio? Pryd maen nhw'n eu gwisgo nhw? Ydy'r label yn bwysig?

Gweithgareddau posibl sy'n deillio o'r wybodaeth

- Estyn y cyfeiriad ar ddiwedd y darn, sy'n dweud bod jîns yn boblogaidd iawn heddiw, i drafod dillad ffasiynol, cyfwisgoedd ffasiynol ac ati.

- Cynllunio jîns / dillad arbennig a'u hysbysebu (ar gyfer cylchgrawn / y teledu ac ati).

- Ymchwilio er mwyn gweld a oes dillad eraill wedi cael eu henwi ar ôl pobl (e.e. leotard, *wellingtons*, cardigan, *bloomers*); cymharu gwybodaeth. Gellir gwneud hyn drwy deipio *eponym* i beiriant chwilio ar y rhyngrwyd.

- Ymchwilio er mwyn gweld pa bethau eraill sydd wedi eu henwi ar ôl pobl arbennig. Gellir gwneud hyn drwy deipio *eponym* i beiriant chwilio ar y rhyngrwyd.

Siocled ...siocled ... a mwy o siocled!: Teulu Cadbury (tt. 9-11)

Gallech chi ddechrau drwy:

- drafod pa siocled mae'r disgyblion yn ei fwyta; Pryd? Pa mor aml? Pam? ac ati

- gwneud holiadur i weld faint o siocled mae'r disgyblion yn ei fwyta, pwy sy'n bwyta fwyaf ac ati
- cynllunio rysáit newydd ar gyfer siocled.

Gweithgareddau posibl sy'n deillio o'r wybodaeth

- Chwilio am fwy o wybodaeth am siocled *Cadbury's*, e.e. pa fathau sy'n cael eu gwerthu heddiw, faint maen nhw'n gostio ac ati.
- Cynllunio hysbyseb am *Cadbury's*, e.e. hysbyseb 'hen ffasiwn' i ddangos beth roedd y cwmni'n arfer ei werthu, hysbyseb fodern i hyrwyddo cynnyrch heddiw (e.e. hysbyseb ar bapur ar gyfer y cynnyrch gwreiddiol, mewn lliwiau addas, hysbyseb gyffrous ar gyfer y radio neu'r teledu heddiw).
- Chwilio am fwy o wybodaeth am *Cadbury's* ar y rhyngrwyd.

Bob Geldof KBE (tt. 12-16)

Gallech chi ddechrau drwy:

- drafod pa fath o gerddoriaeth mae'r disgyblion yn ei hoffi, pam ac ati
- dod â chryno ddisgiau modern i'r wers er mwyn cynnal sesiwn mynegi barn, disgrifio hoff ganwr/band; gallai'r athro/athrawes chwarae un o ganeuon y *Boomtown Rats* a/neu Bob Geldof ei hun er mwyn annog y disgyblion i fynegi barn am y gerddoriaeth
- dangos toriadau papur, darnau ar fideo sy'n ymwneud â Bob Geldof yn siarad dros bobl Affrica, os yw'n briodol
- dangos lluniau o bobl dlawd yn Affrica a llun o Bob Geldof a thrafod y berthynas rhyngddyn nhw
- dangos rhai o'r lluniau yn y llyfr *Geldof in Africa* i'r dosbarth.

Gweithgareddau posibl sy'n deillio o'r wybodaeth

- Chwilio am fwy o wybodaeth am Bob Geldof.
- Gwrando ar fwy o ganeuon y *Boomtown Rats*, e.e. gellid gwrando ar '*I don't like Mondays*', a sôn am yr hanes sy'n gefndir i'r gân. Gellir cael geiriau'r gân a'r hanes ar y rhyngrwyd.

- Chwilio am fwy o wybodaeth am *Live Aid* a *Live Eight*, e.e. pwy yn union oedd yn perfformio, faint o bobl oedd yno, ac ysgrifennu am y digwyddiadau, e.e. erthygl, cyfweliad dychmygol, posteri ac ati.
- Cysylltu ag elusen fel Cymorth Cristnogol, neu *Tearfund* er mwyn cael gwybodaeth ddiweddar am sefyllfa pobl Ethiopia / Affrica; gwahodd siaradwr i'r dosbarth.
- Trafod a chynnal ymgyrch i godi arian at elusen.
- Sôn am y record Gymraeg '*Dwylo Dros y Môr*', dilyn y geiriau a mynegi barn.

J.K. Rowling ... a ... Harry Potter (tt. 17-20)

Gallech chi ddechrau drwy:

- drafod pa fath o lyfrau mae'r disgyblion yn eu mwynhau, pam ac ati
- cynnal cwis Harry Potter, e.e. gallai grwpiau feddwl am gwestiynau i'w gofyn i grwpiau eraill, yna gellid cynnal y cwis, cadw sgôr ac ati
- gofyn i grwpiau feddwl am wahanol fathau o ddeunyddiau hyrwyddo Harry Potter, cymharu gwybodaeth a dangos rhai o'r deunyddiau
- dangos rhan o ffilm Harry Potter a'i thrafod
- gofyn i'r disgyblion oes ganddyn nhw lyfrau Harry Potter - pa rai? Fuodd y disgyblion yn ciwio dros nos i'w prynu nhw? Archebon nhw'r llyfrau o flaen llaw? ac ati.

Gweithgareddau posibl sy'n deillio o'r wybodaeth

- Dangos *Harri Potter a Maen yr Athronydd* i'r dosbarth; dyfalu beth yw ' Wfftipwff', 'Crafangfran', 'Llereurol' a 'Slafennog', ble mae'r 'Lôn Groes' ac ati.
- Mynegi barn am lyfrau / ffilmiau Harry Potter.
- Ysgrifennu hysbyseb / adolygiad o un o'r llyfrau/ffilmiau.
- Egluro bod Harry Potter, fel arwr, yn wahanol iawn i arwyr storïau eraill. Gofyn i bob grŵp feddwl am arwr / arwres hollol newydd, ei ddisgrifio o ran oed, teulu, pryd a gwedd, diddordebau ac ati. Cymharu syniadau. Yna, mewn grŵp, cynllunio ac ysgrifennu stori fer am yr arwr / arwres yma.

Pobl Llyfr 4 Lefelau 6/7

Ceir chwech o unedau am wahanol bobl, sef:

- Sarah Jacob
- Y Jacuzzi: Candido Jacuzzi
- Clarence Birdseye
- Gordon Bennett
- Tri ... ar Drywydd y Tywydd
- Syr Ranulph Fiennes

Sarah Jacob (tt. 3-5)

Gallech chi ddechrau drwy:

- drafod arferion bwyta, e.e.
  - Beth ydych chi'n gael i frecwast / cinio / te / swper?
  - Beth am rwng prydau bwyd?
  - Ydych chi'n bwyta'n iach neu'n afiach?
  - Sut gallwch chi wella'ch diet?

  Yna, gellid symud yn raddol at y syniad o beidio bwyta am gyfnod.
  - Sut ydych chi'n teimlo pan mae eisiau bwyd arnoch chi? (yn wan? / yn flin? / wedi blino? / eisiau eistedd a gwneud dim byd? / eisiau cysgu? / stumog yn gwneud sŵn?)

  Yna, gellid cyflwyno hanes Sarah Jacob.

Gweithgareddau posibl sy'n deillio o'r wybodaeth

- Chwarae rôl, e.e. cyfweld un o'r bobl oedd yn ei gwylio hi.
- Ysgrifennu adroddiad / dyddiadur / erthygl amdani.

- Trafod yr hanes – beth ddigwyddodd?
  - Ydy hi'n bosibl byw heb fwyd am gymaint o amser?
  - Sut llwyddodd Sarah Jacob?
  - Oedd hi'n twyllo? / Oedd ei rhieni hi'n twyllo?

- Os yw'n briodol, gellid trafod salwch sy'n gysylltiedig â pheidio bwyta, e.e. anorecsia neu fwlimia. *Fodd bynnag, bydd angen ystyried aelodaeth y dosbarth yn ofalus, gan sicrhau nad yw'r pwnc yn debygol o fod yn un sensitif i ddisgyblion penodol.*

Y Jacuzzi (tt. 6-8): Candido Jacuzzi

Gallech chi ddechrau drwy:

- drafod sut mae'r disgyblion yn ymlacio, gan arwain at y syniad o gael bath cynnes, ymlaciol, mynd i'r jacuzzi

- gofyn sawl un o'r dosbarth sy wedi bod mewn jacuzzi – sut brofiad oedd e.

Gweithgareddau posibl sy'n deillio o'r wybodaeth

- Edrych ar luniau o jacuzzis / ystafelloedd ymolchi, eu disgrifio a cheisio cael y disgyblion i'w gwerthu i'w gilydd.

- Cynllunio ystafell ymolchi ddelfrydol.

- Trafod pwysigrwydd sawna mewn gwledydd Sgandinafaidd.

- Ymchwilio i offer / celfi eraill yn y tŷ er mwyn gweld o ble daeth y syniad gwreiddiol.

- Ymchwilio er mwyn gweld pa bethau eraill sydd wedi eu henwi ar ôl pobl arbennig. Gellir gwneud hyn drwy deipio *eponym* i beiriant chwilio ar y rhyngrwyd.

Pobl

Clarence Birdseye (tt. 9-11)

Gallech chi ddechrau drwy:

- wneud arolwg i weld faint o fwydydd wedi eu rhewi mae'r disgyblion yn eu bwyta ac yna trafod hyn mewn grŵp

- gwneud arolwg o'r bwydydd yma a'u categoreiddio - pa fath o fwydydd sydd wedi eu rhewi? Bwyd melys? Bwydydd sawrus? Llysiau? Ffrwythau? ac ati.

Gweithgareddau posibl sy'n deillio o'r wybodaeth

- Edrych ar hysbysebion print / ar fideo sy'n hysbysebu bwydydd wedi eu rhewi a'u trafod:
  - Beth maen nhw'n hysbysebu?
  - Pwy maen nhw'n targedu?
  - Ydyn nhw'n hysbysebion da?
  - Pam?

- Gwneud hysbysebion ar gyfer bwyd wedi ei rewi – ar gyfer cylchgrawn / y teledu.

- Dod â phecynnau gwag o fwydydd sydd wedi eu rhewi i'r dosbarth er mwyn eu defnyddio mewn sefyllfa marchnad, e.e. rhaid paratoi sgript i werthu'r bwyd, yna perfformio mewn sefyllfa marchnad, gan ddangos y pecyn a gweiddi er mwyn cael sylw, e.e.

  'Dewch ... Dewch ... Heddiw, mae gen i fargen arbennig iawn i chi ... Mae'n rhatach na'r siopau ...'

Gordon Bennett (tt. 12-14)

Gallech chi ddechrau drwy:

- ddangos lluniau o gylchgronau sy'n dangos selebs yn cael amser da, trafod pwy ydyn nhw, ble maen nhw, beth maen nhw'n wneud ac ati. Yna, egluro bod James Gordon Bennett yn mwynhau bywyd a'i fod yn dipyn o *playboy*.

Gweithgareddau posibl sy'n deillio o'r wybodaeth

- Chwilio am fwy o wybodaeth am ras falŵns Gordon Bennett.
- Chwilio am fwy o wybodaeth am rasys TT Ynys Manaw.
- Gofyn i bawb feddwl am rywbeth gwirion maen nhw wedi wneud, ysgrifennu am y digwyddiad, cymharu syniadau.

Tri ... ar Drywydd y Tywydd (tt. 15-16)

Gallech chi ddechrau drwy:

- wylio rhagolygon y tywydd yn Gymraeg ar fideo, trafod y tywydd; byddai'n braf gwylio'r rhagolygon o'r noson gynt, trafod oedd y rhagolygon yn gywir, pa mor aml mae pobl y tywydd yn gywir, tybed.

Gweithgareddau posibl sy'n deillio o'r wybodaeth

- Chwilio am fwy o wybodaeth am Helen Willetts, Derek Brockway a Siân Lloyd.
- Gwylio rhaglenni teledu eraill lle mae'r tri yma'n ymddangos, e.e. Plant mewn Angen, *Risg*.
- Gwneud ymchwil er mwyn gweld sut mae pobl y tywydd yn paratoi bwletin y tywydd.
- Paratoi rhagolygon y tywydd am ddau neu dri diwrnod – eu cyflwyno a'u ffilmio/recordio.

Syr Ranulph Fiennes (tt. 17-20)

Gallech chi ddechrau drwy:

- ddarllen penawdau (yn Saesneg efallai) yn cyflwyno prif gampau Syr Ranulph; gofyn i grwpiau nodi ar ddarn o bapur beth maen nhw'n ei wybod am Syr Ranulph

- gofyn i ddisgyblion ymchwilio / cywain gwybodaeth am Syr Ranulph, cymharu gwybodaeth
- cyflwyno rhai o lyfrau Syr Ranulph.

Gweithgareddau posibl sy'n deillio o'r wybodaeth

- Paratoi cyfweliad gyda Syr Ranulph yn seiliedig ar y darn darllen a'r wybodaeth a gafwyd uchod.
- Ymchwilio ymhellach i agweddau penodol e.e. dinas goll Ubar.
- Edrych yn benodol ar yr ymgyrchoedd codi arian, mynegi barn arnyn nhw a cheisio meddwl am ymgyrch llawn her, anturus arall ar gyfer codi arian.
- Ymchwilio er mwyn cael gwybodaeth am bobl eraill sydd wedi teithio'n bell / sydd wedi cyflawni camp arbennig, e.e. Capten Scott – mae cerflun iddo ym Mae Caerdydd a chloc coffa iddo ef a'i gyfeillion ym Mharc y Rhath, Caerdydd.